Plutarch's treatise upon the distinction between a friend and flatterer: with remarks. By Thomas Northmore, ...

Plutarch

Plutarch's treatise upon the distinction between a friend and flatterer: with remarks. By Thomas Northmore, ...
Plutarch
ESTCID: T107372
Reproduction from British Library
With a divisional titlepage and a final advertisement leaf.
London : printed for Payne; Egertons; Deighton; and Shepperson and Reynolds, 1793.
vii,[1],84,[2],85-132,[2]p. ; 8°

Eighteenth Century
Collections Online
Print Editions

Gale ECCO Print Editions

Relive history with *Eighteenth Century Collections Online*, now available in print for the independent historian and collector. This series includes the most significant English-language and foreign-language works printed in Great Britain during the eighteenth century, and is organized in seven different subject areas including literature and language; medicine, science, and technology; and religion and philosophy. The collection also includes thousands of important works from the Americas.

The eighteenth century has been called "The Age of Enlightenment." It was a period of rapid advance in print culture and publishing, in world exploration, and in the rapid growth of science and technology – all of which had a profound impact on the political and cultural landscape. At the end of the century the American Revolution, French Revolution and Industrial Revolution, perhaps three of the most significant events in modern history, set in motion developments that eventually dominated world political, economic, and social life.

In a groundbreaking effort, Gale initiated a revolution of its own: digitization of epic proportions to preserve these invaluable works in the largest online archive of its kind. Contributions from major world libraries constitute over 175,000 original printed works. Scanned images of the actual pages, rather than transcriptions, recreate the works ***as they first appeared.***

Now for the first time, these high-quality digital scans of original works are available via print-on-demand, making them readily accessible to libraries, students, independent scholars, and readers of all ages.

For our initial release we have created seven robust collections to form one the world's most comprehensive catalogs of 18th century works.

Initial Gale ECCO Print Editions collections include:

> ### History and Geography
> Rich in titles on English life and social history, this collection spans the world as it was known to eighteenth-century historians and explorers. Titles include a wealth of travel accounts and diaries, histories of nations from throughout the world, and maps and charts of a world that was still being discovered. Students of the War of American Independence will find fascinating accounts from the British side of conflict.

Social Science
Delve into what it was like to live during the eighteenth century by reading the first-hand accounts of everyday people, including city dwellers and farmers, businessmen and bankers, artisans and merchants, artists and their patrons, politicians and their constituents. Original texts make the American, French, and Industrial revolutions vividly contemporary.

Medicine, Science and Technology
Medical theory and practice of the 1700s developed rapidly, as is evidenced by the extensive collection, which includes descriptions of diseases, their conditions, and treatments. Books on science and technology, agriculture, military technology, natural philosophy, even cookbooks, are all contained here.

Literature and Language
Western literary study flows out of eighteenth-century works by Alexander Pope, Daniel Defoe, Henry Fielding, Frances Burney, Denis Diderot, Johann Gottfried Herder, Johann Wolfgang von Goethe, and others. Experience the birth of the modern novel, or compare the development of language using dictionaries and grammar discourses.

Religion and Philosophy
The Age of Enlightenment profoundly enriched religious and philosophical understanding and continues to influence present-day thinking. Works collected here include masterpieces by David Hume, Immanuel Kant, and Jean-Jacques Rousseau, as well as religious sermons and moral debates on the issues of the day, such as the slave trade. The Age of Reason saw conflict between Protestantism and Catholicism transformed into one between faith and logic -- a debate that continues in the twenty-first century.

Law and Reference
This collection reveals the history of English common law and Empire law in a vastly changing world of British expansion. Dominating the legal field is the *Commentaries of the Law of England* by Sir William Blackstone, which first appeared in 1765. Reference works such as almanacs and catalogues continue to educate us by revealing the day-to-day workings of society.

Fine Arts
The eighteenth-century fascination with Greek and Roman antiquity followed the systematic excavation of the ruins at Pompeii and Herculaneum in southern Italy; and after 1750 a neoclassical style dominated all artistic fields. The titles here trace developments in mostly English-language works on painting, sculpture, architecture, music, theater, and other disciplines. Instructional works on musical instruments, catalogs of art objects, comic operas, and more are also included.

biblio life
old books. new life.

The BiblioLife Network

This project was made possible in part by the BiblioLife Network (BLN), a project aimed at addressing some of the huge challenges facing book preservationists around the world. The BLN includes libraries, library networks, archives, subject matter experts, online communities and library service providers. We believe every book ever published should be available as a high-quality print reproduction; printed on-demand anywhere in the world. This insures the ongoing accessibility of the content and helps generate sustainable revenue for the libraries and organizations that work to preserve these important materials.

The following book is in the "public domain" and represents an authentic reproduction of the text as printed by the original publisher. While we have attempted to accurately maintain the integrity of the original work, there are sometimes problems with the original work or the micro-film from which the books were digitized. This can result in minor errors in reproduction. Possible imperfections include missing and blurred pages, poor pictures, markings and other reproduction issues beyond our control. Because this work is culturally important, we have made it available as part of our commitment to protecting, preserving, and promoting the world's literature.

GUIDE TO FOLD-OUTS MAPS and OVERSIZED IMAGES

The book you are reading was digitized from microfilm captured over the past thirty to forty years. Years after the creation of the original microfilm, the book was converted to digital files and made available in an online database.

In an online database, page images do not need to conform to the size restrictions found in a printed book. When converting these images back into a printed bound book, the page sizes are standardized in ways that maintain the detail of the original. For large images, such as fold-out maps, the original page image is split into two or more pages

Guidelines used to determine how to split the page image follows:

- Some images are split vertically; large images require vertical and horizontal splits.
- For horizontal splits, the content is split left to right.
- For vertical splits, the content is split from top to bottom.
- For both vertical and horizontal splits, the image is processed from top left to bottom right.

840 ff. 17

PLUTARCH'S TREATISE

UPON THE DISTINCTION

BETWEEN

A FRIEND AND FLATTERER

WITH

REMARKS.

BY THOMAS NORTHMORE, ESQ. M A F S A

LONDON

PRINTED FOR PAYNE, MEWS-GATE, EGERTONS, WHITEHALL,
DEIGHTON, HOLBORN, AND SHEPPERSON AND REYNOLDS,
OXFORD-STREET

1793

Omnes homines, qui sese student præstare cæteris animalibus, summa ope niti decet, ne vitam silentio transeant, *veluti pecora.*   SALLUST.

To an active mind, indolence is more painful than labour.   GIBBON.

To my valued Friend and Brother-in law,

WILLIAM EARLE WELBY JUN ESQ

Of Carlton House, Nottinghamshire

THERE is no Object so desirable, no Good so beneficial to Man, as the Company of a virtuous Woman. That amiable Softneſs and commanding Modesty inherent in the female Character, not only mitigate the rugged Harshness of our Features, and temper the Severity of our Manners, but preserve us in the Paths of moral Rectitude, and deter us from those of Vice and Errour. From the Loss of such a Companion, in whom every conjugal every amiable Virtue shone with superiour Lustre, it is no small Consolation to me that I can turn for Relief to Friends, whose Hearts I know from Experience to be the

Habitation of Integrity, Sincerity, and Honour. Among these a Writer naturally inscribes his Work, particularly when that Work treats upon Friendship, to one with whom he is more intimately connected; and as Cicero remarked upon a similar Occasion to his Atticus, so may I remark to You, " that in contemplating " the Portrait of a true Friend as de- " lineated in the following Pages, you " cannot be at a Loss to discover your " own." Expressing then an earnest Wish, that an Intimacy now for Years established may continue unabated while we have any Part left to act in this Drama of Life,

I remain
Your affectionate Brother,
THOMAS NORTHMORE.

London, Oct. 28, 1793

TO THE READER.

ALTHOUGH the truth of the Greek adage, *that a great book is a great evil*, be indisputable, yet in my opinion the evil is exceeded by a *great preface*. I have therefore waved my original design of writing a politico-moral preamble, and shall confine myself only to those points, which I deem necessary for every reader to be made acquainted with

The very essential and almost universal advantages held out to us by this treatise, were the chief motives that induced me to undertake a new translation of it, but it is principally to the rich and powerful, to Ministers and Nobles, that the greatest profit can be expected to accrue. It is to them, as leeches to the body, that parasites and flatterers adhere and it is from their blood that they thrive and prosper.

In order therefore to render the work as intelligible as possible, I have made no scruple of adopting any phrase, sentence or words out of the old translation, that seemed adapted to my purpose and herein I expect not to be accused of plagiarism even by my enemies, for if they will take the trouble to compare the two versions together, they will perceive that I have done much; if my abilities had corresponded with my inclination, I would have done more

In the remarks at the end, my labours have for the most part been directed to the promotion and confirmation of the moral doctrines of Plutarch, by bringing them into comparison with those of Cicero in his admirable treatise upon Friendship, the translation of which, by the elegant and accomplished Mr. Melmoth, being held in such merited esteem, I have chosen to adopt, without always reverting to the original.

I have now, Reader, nothing further to inform you of; but hope that you will make a good use of what is presented to you. With respect to myself, my misfortunes have taught me the real value of Philosophy and I say with Cicero, "that there " is a satisfaction in communicating useful ' knowledge of every kind, which renders " any man happy, who employs the talents

" of his mind to so noble and beneficial a
" purpose ' Yes, " it is in endeavouring
" (as Montesquieu rightly observes) to in-
" struct mankind, that we are best able to
" practise that general virtue which com-
" prehends the love of all.'

Farewell.

PLUTARCH'S TREATISE, &c.

TO ANTIOCHUS PHILOPAPPUS.

It is remarked by Plato, my friend, that all men are inclined to regard as venial a more than ordinary share of self-love [1], and yet such a propensity is attended with this bad consequence, beside several others, that it incapacitates us from making an upright and unbiassed judgement of ourselves, for love is blind to the imperfections of the object beloved where we are not accustomed to reverence and pursue that conduct which is honourable and virtuous in preference to that of private interest and affection [2] And hence we lay ourselves open to the arts and machinations of the flatterer who possesses in this our self-fondness a citadel whence he may make his attacks upon us, well knowing that every self-lover, being the first and greatest self-flatterer, admits without difficulty another who he thinks will approve and bear witness to his actions [3] For surely he who is justly reproached with being fond of flattery is also very partial to himself, and through abundance of self-kindness not only wishes to inherit the various perfections which may entitle him to the good opinion of others, but really believes he does so, and though it be laudable enough to encourage the wish, yet we should be very cautious how we indulge in the belief Now if truth, as Plato says, be a particle of the Divinity and the origin of all good to Gods and Men, the flatterer is certainly in danger of being an enemy to the Gods and above all to the Pythian Deity [4]; for he constantly opposes that famous oracle of his—*know thyself*—by teaching every one to deceive himself and keeping him in ignorance of the good and ill qualities that are in him, and thus the former are held in a state of imperfection, and the latter become totally incorrigible

If indeed the flatterer, like most other evils, were to attack only or principally the abject and depraved part of mankind, the matter would neither be of such great importance nor so difficult to be guarded against, but as worms breed and propagate best in tender and sweet wood, so a generosity of manners, and an openness and candour of disposition most easily admit and nourish the flatterer: and moreover as Simonides observes that it is not a small income that will maintain a stud of horses, but a large and ample estate; so we see not flattery the attendant on the poor, the inglorious, or the humble, but we see it the destruction and pest of great wealth and power, and often overthrowing kingdoms and empires: wherefore it is a business of no small moment, nor does it require a little share of forethought, so to investigate its nature that, being detected and brought to light, it may neither injure nor depreciate true friendship. For as vermin forsake the expiring body, the blood by which they were fed being extinguished, so flatterers are not to be seen near the dried and withered scenes of adversity, but stick fast to and thrive and prosper amid riches and honours and powers, and the moment a change takes place they are fled: But it would be imprudent in us to await the experiment, which is not only useless but rather dangerous and hurtful, for surely at a time when we stand most in need of friends it is afflicting to perceive that we are forsaken by those whom we esteemed such, especially when we have it not in our power to substitute a valuable and constant friend in the room of the base and faithless wretch who deserted us. Let us therefore have our friend, as we have our money, well tried and proved before the time of necessity, not convicted in the very act of using him, for it is not enough to feel ourselves injured, but we ought to have so much skill and knowledge of the flatterer that we receive no injury otherwise we shall stand in the same predicament with those who learn the effects of any poisonous and deadly herb from the sad experience of having first tasted it, thus ruining ourselves in improving our judgement.

And as on the one hand we do not applaud such thoughtless and inconsiderate conduct, so on the other we cannot admire that over-nice and cautious disposition, which, measuring friendship only by gravity of deportment and utility, concludes that a pleasant and chearful companion is instantly to be deemed a parasite for a friend is not a morose unsociable animal, nor is friendship venerable only in a severe austerity of manners, but its very gravity and venerable deportment are pleasing and desirable;

> Near it the Graces and sweet Love have fixt
> Their chearful habitations—

Nor indeed, as Euripides observes, is the unfortunate man alone

> Pleased to meet with friendship's soothing eye,

but it increases no less the pleasures and happiness of those who are in prosperity than it diminishes the griefs and sorrows of the afflicted in adversity. And as the philosopher Evenus used to say, " that fire was the best seasoning," so the Almighty, having blended the sweets of friendship with our condition upon earth, hath rendered every thing, when she is present and partakes of it, lovely and agreeable.[6] For how is it possible that the flatterer could put on the mask of pleasantry, if he saw not true friendship cloathed in sweetness? But as gilt and counterfeit vessels imitate the brightness only and splendour of real gold, so the flatterer imitating the sweetness and pleasantry of the friend always shews himself chearful and obliging, and never resists or opposes the gratification of our wishes.

And hence we ought not instantly to suspect those of flattery who praise and commend us, for praise when seasonably applied becomes a true friend no less than censure, nay indeed a perpetually morose and querulous disposition is totally foreign to the pleasing intercourse of real amity, whereas men bear patiently and without murmur the rebuke and admonition of a friend whose benevolence prompts him liberally to bestow on their laudable actions a due degree of commendation, being persuaded that he who is so ready to commend must censure through necessity. It is difficult then, some one may say, to distinguish between the flatterer and the friend, since they differ neither in the pleasure they give nor in the praises they bestow, nay, in various services and performances, we frequently see friendship outstript by flattery.

And why should it not be so, we may answer, if indeed we investigate the character of the real flatterer who handles his business with all possible art and cunning? and not, as the multitude do, rank those trenchermen and parasites as such whose voices, as one said of them, are heard the moment the water is poured upon their hands *, and whose illiberal scurrility and fulsome adulation are made manifest as soon as they have tasted your viands, and cheered themselves with one glass. For certainly there was no necessity to convict Melanthius the parasite of Alexander Pheræus, who upon being asked how Alexander was slain, made answer, " through his side into my stomach " nor indeed those parasites who encircle the tables of the rich ?, whom neither fire nor sword can deter from going to a dinner. nor again those female parasites of Cyprus, who upon passing over into Syria obtained the name of Climacidæ, because by stooping down they made a sort of ladder of their backs for the wives of their patrons to use in ascending their chariots. There is no necessity I say to convict such as these, for their aim is manifest, their whole drift is open and exposed to view. Whom then are we to guard against? The man who neither appears to be false nor stands confest a flatterer, whom we

---

* This was done both before and after meals.

cannot find lurking about our kitchen, nor watching the hour of dinner, who will not upon any occasion indulge in the pleasures of the bottle, but is always sober, meddling and inquisitive, wishes to mix in our affairs and be made a partaker of our secrets [8], and in short rather acts in friendship the grave part of tragedy, than the jocose and cheerful one of comedy. For as Plato says "that it is the summit of injustice to put on the appearance of justice without the substance", so that flattery is to be esteemed most dangerous, which does not act openly but in disguise, which is grave and serious in its deportment, and never relaxes. For such behaviour as this, unless we observe it attentively, fills even the true friend if he often meets with it, with distrust and suspicion, and therefore Gobryas rushing with the impostor Pseudo-Smerdis, whom he was in pursuit of, into a dark room where he had fled, and closing with him, desired his associate Darius, who came in and was hesitating what to do, to thrust them both through. But we who by no means approve of the saying, ' let my friend perish so that my enemy perish with him [9]", but rather wish to separate the flatterer from the friend, connected indeed and entangled with him by too great a similarity, ought to be exceedingly careful that we neither throw away the good with the bad, nor, in our endeavour to preserve the friend, meet by mistake with the enemy. For as the wild grain of the field which bears a great resemblance to the pure wheat both in figure and size, when mixt with it is very difficult to be separated, for either it does not fall through the lesser holes of the sieve, or accompanies the wheat through the larger, so flattery blending itself with friendship in every passion and motion of the mind, and in all intercourse of life and business, is with great difficulty disunited

Now since friendship is the sweetest of all human gratifications, and nothing so much delights and exhilarates mankind, on this account the flatterer clothes himself in pleasures and is totally occupied in administering them and because friendship is constantly attended with mutual acts of kindness and benevolence, as indeed it is said that a friend is more necessary than fire and water [10], therefore the flatterer obtruding himself into our services, strives with the most indefatigable zeal and industry ever to appear attentive to our interest and since a similarity of pursuits and inclinations constitutes chiefly and supports the origin of friendship, and the same aversions and desires first cement and confirm the bands of amity, the flatterer observing this, and being of a very pliable disposition and easily persuaded to put on any appearance, moulds and conforms himself like matter that will receive any impression, seeking only to adjust and regulate his conduct according to the temper of those against whom his designs are formed [11], so as one may say

Is not Achilles' offspring, but Achilles' self.

But the most artful part of his conduct is yet to come, for perceiving that a proper freedom of expostulation is allowed universally to be the very voice and language of real friendship, and as peculiar to it as sound is to any animal, and that a timid behaviour which dares not boldly deliver its sentiments, is repugnant to that liberal openness and sincerity of **heart** which becomes the true friend, he has not let even this escape his imitation but as skilful cooks make use of high seasonings to prevent the stomach being satiated by sweet and luscious meats, so the expostulatory freedom of the flatterer is neither genuine nor useful, but, winking as it were under frowns, tends only to sooth and gratify

Upon these accounts then the flatterer is difficult to be caught, like some animals which, through the bounty of nature, escape pursuit by assuming the colour of the subjacent earth, or herbage that surrounds them [12] But since he deceives us by being disguised under the resemblance of a friend, it is our business to expose and detect him by laying open the difference between them, since he is clothed, as Plato says, in foreign colours and ornaments, having none properly of his own.

Let us consider then this matter from the beginning. We have said that friendship for the most part takes its rise from that similarity of temper and disposition, whereby we embrace the same manners and customs, and delight in the same studies and pursuits [13], according to those lines of the old bard,

> Age is most pleas'd when in sweet converse join'd
> With hoary age, so youth delights in youth,
> And female softneſs harmonizes best
> With kindred tenderneſs, th' infirm th' oppreſt
> Bear to th' oppreſt, th' infirm, a sympathy of woe.

The flatterer then well knowing that all intercourse of love and friendship is grounded in a similitude of passions, here first endeavours to make his approaches, and to pitch his tents, as hunters do in the range and pasture of a wild beast, and here he gradually advances by adapting and accommodating himself to the same pursuits, occupations, studies, and mode of living, untill you are betrayed into his hands, and become mild and familiar to his touch; thus he takes care to censure whatever and whomsoever he perceives to incur your displeasure, and applaud whatever meets your approbation with extravagant fervour, in order that he may appear far to exceed you by his admiration and astonishment, and confirm you in the opinion that his love and hatred arise more from judgement than affection.

How then are we to convict this hypocrite, and by what distinctions is he to be detected, since he does not really resemble the friend, but imitates only his likeness? In the first place we ought to observe the equability and consistency of his life and conduct, whether he delight always in the same objects, and be uniform in his approbations, whether he regulate his behaviour according to one rule, and afford a proper example in his own life, for such conduct alone becomes the free and ingenuous admirer of real and true friendship, such only is the friend: But the flatterer having as it were no one fixt residence of behaviour, nor choosing a life to please himself, but moulding and conforming himself entirely to the will of another, is neither consistent nor uniform, but ever various and changeable, flowing about in every direction, from one shape to another, like water turned out of its course and adapting itself to the soil which receives it. The ape, it seems, is caught while in his endeavours to imitate man, he accompanies his various motions and gestures, but the flatterer allures and attracts others by imitation, though not all in the same manner, for with one he sings and dances, wrestles and boxes with another, and if he chance to fall into the company of any who are fond of hunting and hounds, he scarcely refrains crying out in the words of Phædra,

O how I love to hear the hunter's shouts
Ring through the echoing woods, by the Gods! I love
To hear the full-mouth'd pack, and chace the dappled Stag;

and yet he cares not a rush for the stag, his care only is to entrap the hunter. If indeed he be in pursuit of any young man who is fond of literature, instantly is he enveloped in books, his beard hangs down to his feet [15], his cloak is ragged and threadbare, he is indifferent about every other concern, while the numbers, rectangles, and triangles of Plato are perpetually in his mouth *. If again any rich, idle, debauchee, come in his way,

The wise Ulysses soon strips off his rags,

his threadbare cloak is thrown away, and his beard is mowed down like an unproductive harvest, while he indulges freely in the bottle and the glass, and in ridiculing and scoffing at the philosophers. Thus they say at Syracuse when Plato arrived there and Dionysius was enthusiastic in the study of philosophy, that the whole palace was full of dust and sand on account of the great concourse of Geometricians who described their figures there, but when

* " How much Plato valued mathematical studies, and how
" necessary a preparation he thought them for higher speculations,
" appears from the inscription which he placed over the door
" of his school ᾀυδεὶς ἀγεωμέτρητος εἰσίτω. Let no one who is
" unacquainted with geometry, enter here".
Enfield's Hist of Philosophy B 2 c. 8.

Plato fell into disgrace, and Dionysius forsaking his philosophy betook himself again to drinking, debauchery, and every species of folly and intemperance, instantly were they all transformed as by the cups of Circe, and unlettered barbarism, stupidity and oblivion overwhelmed them. Moreover, the actions of those great flatterers and demagogues who court popular favour, bear witness to what I have asserted, the most noted of whom Alcibiades, while at Athens, indulged his satire and ridicule, kept a stud of horses, and lived a life of urbanity and freedom, at Sparta shaved himself to the skin, put on a worn cloak, and rigidly used the cold bath, the same man in Thrace did nothing but fight and drink, and when he dwelt in Persia with Tissaphernes, was all effeminacy, voluptuousness, and ostentation thus by accommodating himself to the various manners and customs of mankind he gained universal popularity and esteem [16]. Not so Epaminondas, nor Agesilaus, who though conversant with a great variety of men, manners, and states, yet preserved every where the same due and proper decorum, as well in their dress and mode of living as in their words and actions. Thus too was Plato the same man at Syracuse, as at the academy at Athens, and behaved in the same manner to Dionysius as to Dion [17]. But the turns and changes of the flatterer, like those of the polypus [18], are easily discovered, since he is very versatile in his conduct and often alters his appearance, censuring at one time the life which he formerly approved of, and embracing with readiness at another those words and actions that were wont to incur his displeasure. For one shall see him neither firm nor steady in his deportment, nor consistent in his manners, nor does he gratify any passions of his own either in his love and hatred, or joy and sorrow, but, like a mirror, receives the images of foreign humours, habits and affections [19]. Such a man, if you chance to censure any of your friends before him, is ready to say, " you are very late in detecting this fellow, for my part I never once had a good opinion of him". If again you change your sentiments and convert your censure into praise, he will affirm with an oath, " that he heartily congratulates with you, gives credit to every thing you say of the man, and returns you many thanks for his sake". If you talk of altering your course of life, for example, to betake yourself from public business to retirement and ease, " we ought long ago, says he, to have retreated from the tumult and envy of the world" If again you express a wish of coming forward into public life and business, he accords with you and cries out, " now you think worthy of yourself, this retirement certainly has its charms, but is inglorious and ignoble". To such a man you ought instantly to say,

Sure! from thy former self thou art vastly changed:

I want not a friend servilely to comply with all my humours and fancies, and ever be obedient to my nod, for my shadow does as much as this, but I want one who will follow me only in obedience to truth, and assist me impartially with his judgement. Such then is one mode of discovering the flatterer.

But we may observe another distinction in the resemblance he bears to a friend, for a true friend neither praises nor imitates the actions of another indiscriminately, but such only as are truly laudable. According to Sophocles,

> His nature does not lead him servilely
> To copy out your enmity and hate,
> But to partake your friendships and your love,

and indeed to accompany you only in the paths of rectitude and virtue not in the ways of vice and error[20], unless, like some contagious diseases of the eyes, the infection should spread and he should insensibly contract some ill habit by reason of his familiarity and intercourse. As, they say, the companions of Plato learnt to imitate his gibbous shoulders, of Aristotle, his stammering, and of Alexander, the inclination of his neck and roughness of his voice for some people are apt unwittingly to imbibe many bad habits from the lives and manners of their friends. But the flatterer evidently resembles the Chamæleon, which changes itself to every colour but white, for being unable to emulate those virtues which are alone worthy his emulation, he takes care to let no vice or imperfection escape him. And as bad painters, who have not skill enough to express the finer touches of beauty, confine their likenesses to wrinkles, spots and scars, so the flatterer imitates your intemperance, superstition, irascibility, harshness to servants, and mistrust of your familiars and relations, for he is by his own nature prone to ill, and fancies that by copying your vices he is far removed from the appearance of censuring them[21]. For they surely have more the semblance of an enemy, who are ever urging the reformation of their friends, and seem to be dissatisfied with and full of indignation at their faults[22], such conduct as this lost Dion the favour of Dionysius, Samius that of Philip, and Cleomenes that of Ptolemy, and ended in their ruin, but flatterers, being desirous of appearing as well agreeable companions as faithful friends, pretend on account of the violence of their affection to be disgusted not even at your vices but in every respect to labour under the same natural infirmities and passions as yourself.

And hence it is that they disdain not to participate even of the casualties which afflict others, nay indeed they refine upon adulation, and flatter the sick by pretending to have the same diseases;

so that if they meet with men who are rather deaf or blind they can forsooth neither hear nor see well themselves; thus the parasites of Dionysius who was afflicted with a dimness of sight, used to stumble upon each other, and throw down the dishes in the midst of dinner. Others indeed, laying siege to the passions, insinuate themselves deeper, and work their way into your most secret concerns by pretending to be fellow-sufferers. For if they perceive you unhappy in wedlock, or suspicious and distrustful of your children or familiars, they spare not themselves, and entertain you with a lamentable account of the private misfortunes of their own children or wife, or relations or friends, for a similitude of sufferings awakens the sympathy of men, who having, as it were, received pledges of fidelity, divulge their own secrets with greater readiness, this puts them entirely under the power of the flatterer, and they dare not afterwards forsake their trust.[23] I myself knew a man repudiate his wife, because his friend had divorced his, but he was detected, by this friend's wife, frequenting and corresponding with her in private. So little was he acquainted with the nature of flattery who thought that those lines of the poet were meant rather to describe the crab than the flatterer,

> The reptile crawls on teeth, his curious eye
> Pries every where, and his whole body is one paunch,

for this is the very image of a parasite, and of such as Eupolis calls trencher-men and dinner-friends. But these things we will reserve for their proper place.

And in the mean time let us not pass over unnoticed that artifice of the flatterer in his imitation of the friend, wherein, though he imitate some virtue of the person flattered, he takes care always to yield him the superiority [24]. With true friends indeed there is neither envy nor emulation, but whether equal or inferior in doing good the same equanimity and moderation of temper uniformly possess them. But the flatterer, always bearing in his remembrance the inferior parts which he is acting, will never allow himself to be your equal, but confesses that he is every where vanquisht and outstript except in what is bad. In this indeed he yields not the pre-eminence, but affirms that if his friend be of a morose, sour disposition, he himself is quite choked with choler; if superstitiously inclined, he is all enthusiasm; if in love, he loves even to madness; you, says he, have laughed rather immoderately, but I am almost dead with laughter. When any good and useful qualities are the subject of his observation, his behaviour is quite the reverse; he perhaps will allow himself to be swift of foot, but you fly; he manages a horse well, but what in comparison of this hypocentaur! I am a tolerable poet, and my verses are not unharmonious,

But Thunder is Jove's attribute, not mine [25].

Thus he seems to declare his approbation of your studies and pursuits, by imitating them, and at the same time the superiority of your genius, by being vanquisht in the contest

Such then are the distinctions to be made of the flatterer in his counterfeit resemblance of the friend

But since, as I have already remarked, they both partake of the art of pleasing, (for the good man derives no less satisfaction from friends, than the bad one from flatterers) let us discriminate this matter. The method then of discriminating is, by a reference to the end in view, and you may consider it thus There is in various oils a richness of perfume, so also is there in some medicines, but they widely differ, inasmuch as the former have no other object but the gratification of the senses, while the latter are intended to purify, refresh, and invigorate the body, and in other respects are sweet and grateful to the smell Again, the colours and tints used by painters are very florid and beautiful, so there are also some medicinal drugs very grateful to the sight, and salutary too in their use, how then are they to be distinguished? surely by the end to which their uses are directed. In like manner the mutual favours and kind offices of friends carry with them a conspicuous beauty and satisfaction, besides the utility to be derived from them sometimes indeed they partake of the pleasures of the table and the glass, and in good truth often of social mirth and innocent amusements, using these by way of seasoning to their more serious admonitions [26], whence it is said by the Poet,

 And pleasing conference beguiles the day *,
and again,

 There with commutual zeal we both had strove
 In acts of dear benevolence and love †

But the whole business and object of the flatterer is ever to cook and dish up some frolicksome piece of wit or facetious jest solely for the purpose of gratifying the palate. In short, the one has no other end in view but to make himself agreeable, the other, by ever discharging his duty is often agreeable and often harsh and severe, not wishing to be so, but if it be for his friends good, not avoiding it [27]. For as a physician will sometimes for the benefit of his patient, add to other ingredients nard and saffron, and recommend a moderate use of the bath, and a mild and pleasant diet, at other times omitting these lenient measures is wont to throw in castor,

 Or poley most offensive to the smell,

* Pope Il. xi. 788.   † Ib. Odys. iv. 241.

or perhaps compels him to drink off an infusion of hellebore, yet neither making in the one case the disagreeable, nor in the other the agreeable, the object of his pursuit, but leading the patient to one end by both means so the friend sometimes spurs on his companion to virtue, by shewing him marks of favour, and extolling him with praise and commendation, as in the following lines of the poet,

> Oh! youth for ever dear, the monarch cried,
> Thus, always thus, thy early worth be tried·
> Thy brave example shall retrieve our host,
> Thy country's saviour, and thy father's boast *.

And in another place,

> How can I doubt, while great Ulysses stands
> To lend his counsels, and assist our hands †?

At other times, when there is need of reprimand, he chides him with a provident and salutary freedom of admonition and reproof,

> Whither O Menelaus would'st thou run,
> And tempt a fate, w'uch prudence bids thee shun?
> Griev'd though thou art, forbear the rash design,
> Great Hector's arm is mightier far than thine ‡

Sometimes indeed he unites action to words, as Menedemus reclaimed the prodigal and dissolute son of his friend Asclepiades by debarring him from his presence, and not deigning to speak

* Pope Il viii 339   † Ib Il x. 285.   ‡ Ib Il vii 127.

a word to him: and Arcesilaus excluded Battus from his school, because he had traduced Cleanthes in a comedy, but was afterwards reconciled to him upon his repentance, and making a proper satisfaction to Cleanthes. For though it may be our duty to afflict our friend for his advantage, yet we ought not so to afflict him as to destroy friendship, but should rather apply our reproof and censure as a medicine that may cure and preserve the patient.[28] And hence a true friend harmonizing as it were, and modulating his changes according to what is useful and honourable, at one time relaxing and at another increasing his tension, is often pleasing and agreeable, and at all times serviceable. Whereas the flatterer by being ever accustomed to sound in one and the same strain, that only which is meant to please and gratify the senses, knows not how to act or speak in opposition to your desires or inclinations, but is subservient to your will alone, taking care ever to be in unison and concert with you. And as Xenophon says that Agesilaus was delighted with the praise of those, who were not unwilling, when a proper occasion presented itself, to censure him; so ought we to esteem him as our true friend who, though ready to soothe and gratify us, will also sometimes oppose our wishes and resist our inclinations: whereas that intercourse and behaviour which are constant in their endeavours to please and delight, without any mixture of severity, ought surely to be had in suspicion, nor would it be amiss to have always in readiness the saying of the Spartan (Archidamidas), who, upon hearing some one praise Charilaus (king of Sparta) for his universal mildness, said, " How can this man " be so good who finds no fault even with the " wicked?" The gadfly, they say, penetrates into the ears of oxen, and the tick into those of dogs, and the flatterer holding the ears of the ambitious by his praises, and sticking fast to them, is very difficult to be rubbed off

It behoves us therefore, when these parasites are lavishing their praises, to keep our judgement carefully on the watch, and observe well whether the commendation bestowed be intended for the action or the man, and it is for the former, if they praise us rather in our absence than in our presence, if too they be desirous themselves of cultivating the same qualities, they emulate not only us, but all in similar circumstances, nor do they ever pursue either in their language or practice, a conduct that is inconsistent with, or contradictory to their own professions But what ought principally to be observed is, whether we be ourselves conscious that we neither repent nor are ashamed of those things for which we are flattered, nor are desirous of having said or done the contrary, for our sacred monitor within witnessing against us, and neither expecting nor deserving the praise received, is unaffected by it and impregnable to the arts of the flatterer. But, I know not how it is, the generality of mankind do not so easily admit of comfort in their misfortunes, as they are led away by those who join and associate in their sorrows and lamentations [29], and upon the commission of any fault or error, the man who excites a penitential conviction of conscience by a proper rebuke and censure, is instantly deemed a calumniator and an enemy, while he who applauds and approves what is done, is readily embraced as a kind and true friend [30].

Those parasites indeed, who instantly accompany with their plaudits and commendations, any word or action of another, whatever it may be, whether in jest or earnest, are hurtful only at the moment, whereas they who penetrate to the morals by their praises, and affect the very manners by their adulation, are as bad as those domestic robbers who steal not from the heap in the granary, but pilfer even that which is reserved for seed. For the morals and disposition, which are the seed of actions, the origin and fountain of life, are corrupted and perverted by vice being cloathed in the garb of virtue. Thucydides remarks, that in wars and seditions, men are wont to change the customary signification of words according to their own wills and inclinations, for a rash, headstrong boldness, is called fortitude and patriotism, a considerate and cautious delay, is a specious name for cowardice, modesty is the pretext of fear, and a constant prudence and circumspection, are thought inactivity and sloth. So also among flatterers we may observe that profuseness is termed liberality, cowardice, caution, a senseless temerity, acuteness of genius, sordid parsimony, frugality, an amorous youth receives the appellation of tender and affectionate, one that is passionate and proud is deemed brave and manly, and the low and vulgar are humane and affable. Thus Plato somewhere remarks that a lover, who is always a flatterer of the object beloved, stiles the flat nose handsome, the aquiline, princely, that a swarthy complexion shews with him manliness and strength, that those who are fair and white are the children of the Gods, and that the appellation of honey-coloured, is the peculiar phrase of a lover who would flatter and compliment the paleness of his beloved.

Now though a deformed person who is persuaded that he is handsome, or one of low stature that he is tall does not remain long under the delusion, and the injury which he receives is but trifling and not irremediable, yet that praise which habituates a man equally to the practice of vice as of virtue not only without disgust but with satisfaction, and which moreover takes away from sinful actions all shame and remorse, such adulation as this, I say, destroyed the Sicilians by veiling the tyranny of Dionysius and Phalaris under the specious names of justice and abhorrence of vice: it was this that ruined Egypt by denominating the effeminacy, enthusiasm, howlings, and lamentations, and superstitious practices of Ptolemy, true piety and reverence for the gods [31] this too had very nearly overturned and destroyed the morals of the Romans by softening the luxury, intemperance, profuse public entertainments of Anthony under the appellation of generous and noble deeds, well worthy a man whom power and fortune had favoured liberally and without envy. For what fastened on Ptolemy his pipe and flute? What affixed to Nero the tragic stage, and put on his mask and buskin? Was it not the praise of sycophants and flatterers? And are not the generality of princes and great men saluted with the name of Apollo if they do but whine? Bacchus, if they get drunk? And Hercules, if they can but wrestle or box [32]? And are they not delighted with such fulsome adulation, and led away by it to all manner of disgrace and shame?

Surely then it concerns us much to guard against the praises of the flatterer, and this he seems very sensible of, as he carefully avoids every thing that tends to suspicion. If indeed he meet with some well-dressed fop or a dull and stupid country clown, he instantly plays off his wit, as Struthias derided Bias and mocked and ridiculed his stupidity by these ironical praises,

———— Not Alexander's self
Could drink so much [33].

And again,

In laughter you surpass the Cyprian [34]

But when he observes men more shrewd and watchful, and upon their guard against his irony, he does not bring up his flattery in a direct line, but winding about encircles and approaches them gradually, as if he were very cautiously tempting and handling some animal, for at one time he will inform a man of the praises and commendations which others bestow upon him, introducing like the Rhetoricians some third person, and telling him that he very happily entered into conversation with some elders or strangers in the Forum, who made very honourable mention of him, and admired his virtues At another time feigning some false and trivial charges against him and putting them well together, he comes up to him in great haste, as if he had just heard them from others, and asks him whether he ever did this thing or said that? and upon his answering in the negative, as in all probability he would do, the flatterer immediately holds him fast and entangles him in his praises " I was wondering " indeed, says he, that you should have spoken

"ill of any of your friends, who are not accus-
"tomed so to treat your enemies, that you, who
"are so liberal in giving away your own pro-
"perty, should have invaded that of your neigh-
"bours." Others indeed, like painters who increase the lustre of the bright and luminous parts
of a picture by contrasting them with the dark
and shady, secretly cherish and commend the
vices of those they flatter by reviling, calumniat-
ing, or ridiculing the opposite virtues. Thus
among debauchees, extortioners, workers of fraud
and deceit, and men who become rich from
wicked and disgraceful means, these parasites rail
at temperance and modesty as mere rusticity, and
contentment with one's own and love of justice
are abused by them as marks of a timorous spirit
and a want of vigour for action. When indeed
they are conversant with men of a slothful and
indolent disposition, who love to live at their
ease, and avoid all intercourse with business, they
are not ashamed to call the administration of
public affairs a laborious toil for other men,
and a laudable ambition is termed with them a
fruitless love of empty praise. Sometimes with
rhetorical adulation they calumniate and vilify
the philosopher, and find favour with impudent
and lascivious women by reviling the chaste
wife who loves her husband, as a rustic without
passion.

But the most artful and iniquitous part of their conduct is that they abstain not even from vilifying themselves, for as wrestlers lower their own bodies the more easily to throw down their adversaries, so flatterers by exposing their own failings glide down into the admiration of others' virtues "I am a great coward, says the parasite, "where there is the least appearance of danger. "I abhor and protest against all labour and toil, "and if any thing ill is spoken of me, am quite "furious with rage and passion, but to my friend "here nothing is formidable, nothing is grievous "or irksome, but he is a man of a singular and "happy turn of mind, and bears every evil with "great patience and equanimity." If the person flattered should happen to entertain a high opinion of his own abilities, and wish to be thought a man of a grave and serious deportment, and very rigid and inflexible in his manners, and should with some propriety perpetually hold up to view that line of the poet,

It fits thee not to praise me or to blame*,

The artful flatterer does not approach him in the same manner, but adopts another contrivance, for he comes to consult with him about his own private affairs as with one of superior judgement, and says, that though he has other friends with

* Pope Il x 291.

whom he is more intimate, yet he is through necessity compelled to trouble him For where shall we fly who stand in need of counsel or to whom shall we trust? As soon as he has received the answer, whatever it may be, he goes away declaring that he has obtained the response of an oracle, and not the suggestions of human wisdom. If indeed he perceive a man affecting some skill in literature, he gives him one of his own compositions and requests him to revise and correct it And when Mithridates (King of Pontus) was studying the arts of physic and surgery, some of his parasites, who wished to carry their adulation beyond mere words, gave him up their own bodies to make his experiments upon, for by thus trusting themselves in his hands they seemed to bear evident witness to his skill.

> So manifold and various are the forms
> Which evil men put on

But this species of negative praise, though it requires greater caution and circumspection on our part, is nevertheless discoverable by purposely giving the flatterer some absurd and unseasonable advice, and making some trifling and impertinent corrections, for if he shews no opposition to what you say, but approves and admits of all your decisions, and exclaims at each, "how "excellent! how admirably well!" it is evident that

> He asks advice but plays another game,

and studies only to puff you up with praise and adulation. Moreover, as some philosophers have described painting to be mute poetry, so also is there a species of silent adulation as expressive as the loudest encomium: for as hunters more easily deceive the game which they are in pursuit of by appearing engaged in some other business, whether that of cultivating the ground, feeding cattle, or travelling on the road, so the praises of the flatterer have then the surest hold, when he appears least to commend you. For surely he who resigns his seat or couch upon the entrance of another, or, while haranguing before the people or in council, breaks off instantly his discourse and delivers up the rostrum, upon perceiving any rich and powerful man desirous of speaking, surely I say such an one shews more clearly by his silence, than by any exclamation whatever, in how superior a light he views the other's judgement and virtues.

And hence it is that we observe these sycophants and parasites seizing upon the first seats in the theatres and auditories, not that they imagine themselves worthy of such honour, but solely with a view to ingratiate themselves with the rich, by resigning their places. Hence too we may see them beginning an oration in the assemblies of the people and public councils, but instantly retracting their opinions, and readily yielding them up as to their superiors, if perchance any rich, powerful, or great man should happen to oppose them. Wherefore it is our duty to reprove and correct such parasitical concessions and deferences, inasmuch as they are paid neither to experience, nor virtue, nor age, but solely to riches and honours.[5] Thus was Megabyzus (a priest of Diana) reproved by the celebrated Apelles, for, being once in his painting room, and desirous of entering into a discourse about lines and shades, " Do you see, said the great painter, " those boys there grinding colours? while you ' held your peace they looked up to you with " wonder, and admired your gold and purple, " but now that you begin to talk of things which " you do not understand, they ridicule, and de-" spise you[36]." And Solon, having been asked by Crœsus (king of Lydia) whether he ever knew a happier man than himself, declared that one Tellus an obscure citizen of Athens, and Bito, and Cleobis, were much happier. But flatterers pronounce princes, rich men, and rulers not only blessed and happy, but assert that they excel in wisdom, in science, and in every kind of virtue. Some men indeed can not bear to hear the maxim of the Stoics who affirm that the wise man is at the same time rich, noble, generous, and a prince but flatterers surely are less to be borne who attribute to the rich man not only the qualifications of the rhetorician and poet, but if he please, those of the painter and musician, they declare him likewise to be swift of foot, and of great strength, and shew their adulation by suffering themselves to be overcome at a wrestling match, and outstript in the race thus Crisson the Himeræan, in a contest with Alexander, purposely suffered the king to outrun him, but the king perceived it, and was much enraged. Carneades* used to say, that the children of rich and great men learn only one thing well, which is *riding*; for the tutor extols and flatters them in the schools, and they who engage in the gymnastic exercises with them take care to be overcome, but the horse who neither knows nor cares whether his rider be a private subject, or one in power, rich or poor, soon disengages himself from the man who is unable to manage him [37]. Therefore it was very absurdly and foolishly said by Bion, that, "if a man " could by praising a piece of ground make it fer- " tile and productive, he would not seem more " blameable by so doing, than he would by dig- " ging and cultivating it so likewise would there " be no absurdity in one man's praising another, " if by so doing he could be of any advantage " and utility to that other.' Such a speech, I say, is foolish, because a piece of ground does not become worse by any commendations that are

* Carneades was a native of Cyrene, and founder of the New Academy. For his life and doctrine see Enfield's Hist of Philosophy Book II Ch VIII § 2.

bestowed upon it, whereas a man by false and unmerited praise is often puffed up and ruined

Let this suffice for the present subject. We will now proceed to treat of freedom in reprehension. For as Patroclus, when he put on the armour of Achilles, and drove his steeds to the battle, forbore to touch his massive spear, so should the flatterer, though adorned and decorated with all the other insignia and symbols of the friend, abstain from, and not dare to imitate that plain and open frankness, which is, as it were, a conspicuous weapon of friendship,

<blockquote>Huge, weighty, strong [38].</blockquote>

But since these parasites, in order to avoid reprehension in the jollity of convivial moments and amidst scoffs and jests, become affectedly grave upon any matter, and flatter with a sourness and severity upon their countenance, and blend also some degree of censure and admonition in their discourse, let us not pass over this subject without some examination.

It seems to me then that, as in the comedy of Menander a false Hercules is introduced wielding a club that is neither solid nor ponderous, but some light, hollow, counterfeit resemblance of one, so the freedom and boldness of the parasite will appear upon trial to be soft and without weight or vigour: and moreover as the pillows used by the women the more they seem to oppose and resist the head, the more they yield and give way, so this fictitious frankness is elevated and puffed up by a false, empty, and fallacious tumour, in order that by contracting and falling-in it may receive and draw into its own bosom every one who trusts to it For the true and genuine admonition of a friend fixes upon real crimes, and though it creates grief and sorrow, yet they are such as are wholesome and salutary, thus indeed it afflicts and cleanses the mind, as honey does the ulcers of the body, but is in other respects serviceable and agreeable. But concerning this I shall be more particular hereafter.

Whereas the flatterer affects to be severe, morose, and inflexible in his dealings with all others, except him against whom his designs are formed for he is harsh and cruel to his domestics, reprimands very sharply the failings of his relatives and acquaintance, neither admires nor reverences any one else, but holds every one in contempt, of an inexorable disposition, leaving no species of malice or slander untouched in exciting others to anger and revenge, for by these means he expects to acquire the character of being an enemy to vice, inasmuch as he is by no means sparing in his censures[39], and does not strive to ingratiate himself by any servile adulation. But with respect to his friend, he pretends to be totally ignorant of any of his great and real crimes, while he is very acute in discerning and very severe in reprimanding any trifling and insignificant failing, as for instance, if any part of his furniture be misplaced, or if he live less commodiously than he might do, if he appear rather negligent in his person or dress, or if his dog or horse be not properly looked after, and such like, but a disrespectful and contemptuous behaviour towards his parents, neglect of his children, dishonourable treatment of his wife, a proud haughty carriage towards his acquaintance, and profusion of his substance, are of no moment or concern to the flatterer, but upon such matters as these he is quite dumb and spiritless like a master of gymnastic exercises, who suffers his wrestler to indulge in drinking and debauchery, but is very severe with him about his oil-flask and strigil*, or a schoolmaster who chides his scholar about his style and tables†, but pays no attention to the solecisms and barbarisms of his language. For the temper and disposition of the parasite are such that he will not say a word to the discourse of an orator, be he ever so wretched or contemptible, but will blame him for his delivery, and severely chide him for spoiling his articulation by drinking cold water, and if he be desired to overlook and correct some ill-written treatise, he will find fault with the thickness of

* An instrument used in the gymnastic exercises, for the purpose of scraping the body previous to its being anointed. It was used also in bathing.

† Or in modern language, pen and paper. The style was a pointed instrument, with which they wrote formerly upon tables of wax.

the paper, and call the writer a dirty negligent fellow. Thus when Ptolemy appeared to be given to literature his minions would wrangle and dispute with him even to midnight about the propriety of some obscure word, some little sentence, or trifling piece of history, but when he exercised the most shameful severities upon the people, scourging them with rods, and loading them with taxes [40], there was not one who dared to oppose or resist such great and oppressive evils. Just then as a man who should use the surgeon's knife in cutting the hair and paring the nails of one who labours under imposthumes and fistulas, so these parasites practise their boldness upon those parts only which produce neither pain nor anguish.

But there are others who far exceed these in artifice and cunning, and accommodate their censures and admonitions to the purpose of pleasing. Thus Agis the Argive, upon Alexander's making some large present to one of his buffoons, exclaimed through envy and vexation, " O what absur-
" dity," and the king turning angrily towards him and asking, " What is it you say?" " Why truly
" I confess, returns he, that I am not a little
" grieved, and take it much to heart seeing that
" all you who are sprung from a divine origin,
" have equal delight in flatterers and buffoons:
" for Hercules took pleasure in certain Cerco-

"pians*, and Bacchus in his Satyrs, and such
"men too are to be seen flourishing under your
"favour." And it is said of Tiberius Cæsar that, coming once into the senate, one of his flatterers rose up and declared that it became all free men to speak boldly their sentiments, and neither to dissemble nor conceal any thing that is for the public good. Having thus roused the attention of the whole senate, a dead silence ensuing, and Tiberius himself anxiously waiting the event, "Hear,
"said he, O Cæsar, what we all accuse you of,
"and no one has yet dared to speak openly his
"sentiments. You are negligent of yourself, and
"expose your person to danger, and wear your-
"self out with cares and troubles for our sakes,
"taking no rest either by night or day." And having gone on much at the same rate, it is reported that Cassius Severus the rhetorician said, "This
"man's boldness will be his ruin."

These indeed are matters of inferior moment, but there are others that are more serious and destructive, particularly where men are not upon their guard. when, for instance, the parasite shall lay to their charge passions and vices directly the reverse of those which they really labour under; as Himerius the flatterer upbraided one of the most

* The Cercopians took great delight in the practice of every species of fraud and deceit, and therefore were said to be changed by Jupiter into apes. Hence the islands Inarime, Prochyte and others which they inhabited, were called Pithecusæ.

illiberal, avaricious misers at Athens for his profuse negligence and prodigality, and telling him that he and his family would one day or other starve, or on the contrary when he reproaches the luxurious and prodigal for their sordid parsimony and avarice, as Titus Petronius did Nero. or when he exhorts those rulers who cruelly and barbarously tyrannize over their subjects to lay aside their too great mildness of disposition, and their unseasonable and useless clemency Not unlike these men is the flatterer who pretends to dread and be on his guard against the dull, stupid fool, as if he were some shrewd and cunning fellow, and who, upon meeting with a man of a malicious and envious temper that takes pleasure in perpetual slander and abuse, will chide and censure him, if perchance he should be induced to commend any meritorious person, as if he laboured under the disease of praising every body, " Your commendations, says he, are bestowed " upon men of no worth, for who is this man or " what has he said or done that merits applause?"

But it is chiefly among lovers and relations that flatterers make their principal assault and do the most harm, for when they see brothers at variance, or children behaving contemptuously towards their parents, or husbands disdainfully treating their wives, they neither use admonition nor censure, but inflame and increase their passions, " You are " not, say they, sufficiently sensible of your own

" importance, and are the cause of all these evils
" by your obsequious and submissive conduct⁴¹.'
But if any quarrel or disagreement should happen
to arise either from anger or jealousy between a
lover and his mistress, the flatterer comes forward
with great boldness, and heaps fuel upon the
flames, pleading the cause of love, and accusing
the lover of many harsh, cruel, and reprehensible
actions,

> O ingrate, and unmindful of the sweet
> And manifold caresses you've receiv'd

Thus the friends of Anthony, who was burning
with love for the Egyptian Queen, persuaded him
that he was adored by her, and reproached him for
his haughtiness and want of affection, " A woman
" here forsaking such a kingdom and so prosper-
" ous a condition is dying for love of you, and
" follows your camp with the appearance of a con-
" cubine,

> " But your hard flinty heart is cas'd in steel,

" and you overlook all her sorrows and afflic-
" tions." And he, highly gratified in thus being
convicted as if he were really guilty of injustice, and
taking that pleasure in his accusers which he would
not have done if they had commended him, did not
perceive that by this counterfeit reprehension he
was the more perverted and depraved. For such
reproof as this is like the bites of lascivious women,
serving only by the seeming pain which it creates

to rouse and irritate the person affected by it. And as wine is in other respects a good antidote against hemlock, but if mixed and blended with it renders the force of the poison irresistible, inasmuch as its circulation to the heart is quickened by the heat of the wine [42], so these evil-minded men, well knowing that freedom of admonition is a great remedy and security against flattery, flatter through its means. Wherefore Bias upon being asked what was the most noxious of animals, did not answer well when he replied, " of the ferocious ones, the tyrant, " of the tame and gentle, the flatterer." For he might have said with greater accuracy, that of flatterers the tame and gentle are those who frequent your bath and your table, but he who extends his busy meddling curiosity, his calumnies and malignant disposition, like so many snakes, into the innermost recesses of your house and family, he is savage, ferocious, and intractable.

Now one method of guarding against such flatterers is always to consider well and remember that, since the soul is composed of two parts, the one, embracing a love of truth and virtue, and an obedience to the dictates of reason, and the other, a disregard of reason, a love of deceit and falsehood, and is subject to the empire of the passions; to remember, that the friend always is the advocate and counsellor to the better part [43], like a physician who confirms and preserves the health of his patient, but the flatterer applies himself closely to the brutish and depraved part which he inflames and irritates, and draws aside from reason by perpetually contriving and suggesting some false and voluptuous pleasures. For as there are some meats which neither coalesce with the blood, nor add any vigour to the spirits, nerves or marrow of the body, but tend only to provoke lust, weaken the stomach, and wither up the flesh, so the flatterer contributes nothing by his discourse to the improvement of the prudent and rational man, but feeds only and cherishes some sensual pleasure, encreases the head-strong violence of passion, stirs up envy, or engenders a vain overbearing haughtiness of mind, heightens the sorrows of another by joining his own tears and lamentations, or inflames the malignity of his temper, his illiberality, and contumacy, and renders them by various shrewd hints and calumnies morose, timorous, and suspicious. By such arts as these the flatterer may always be known, for he constantly takes his station under some one of the passions which he feeds and nourishes, and, like a boil upon the body, grows only upon the diseased and inflamed parts of the mind. Are you angry? revenge yourself, says he. Do you covet any thing? purchase it. Are you afraid? let us fly. Are you suspicious? have confidence. But if we find it difficult to detect him in these insidious attempts upon our passions, because the vehemence and greatness of them often overpower our reason, it will be more easy to discover him in other instances of treachery, for all his actions are of a piece. Thus if at any time you suspect that you have eat too much, and are afraid of a surfeit, and are hesitating whether you should use the bath and take any more food⁴⁴, the true friend endeavours to restrain you, and exhorts you to act with caution, and be upon your guard, but the flatterer drags you forcibly to the bath, and orders another course of dishes to be served up, and not to injure your body by too rigorous a treatment and if at any time he perceive you indolently inclined, and averse to the undertaking of some particular voyage, or journey, or the transacting of some business, he will not advise you not to let slip the present opportunity, but that any other time will do as well, or that the same thing may be done by proxy. But if you have promised to lend or give any friend of yours a sum of money, and afterwards repent of having done so, but are ashamed to forfeit your word, the flatterer immediately throws his own weight into the lighter scale, confirms your opinion in favour of your purse, extirpates every remnant of shame, and advises you to be more sparing, inasmuch as your expences are large, and there are many whom you are desirous of relieving Wherefore if we deceive not ourselves by following our lusts and appetites, by extinguishing shame, and acting in an irresolute, timid manner, the flatterer will never deceive us, for he is always an advocate for such passions as these, and speaks with freedom only when you neglect their sway

Let what I have said suffice for the present subject, and we will now proceed to the various uses and services of friendship For in these particulars the flatterer, by his extreme readiness and willingness to serve you, creates much confusion and renders it difficult to distinguish him from the true friend But as the word of truth, according to Euripides, is simple and unadorned, so the manners of a friend have nothing in them fictitious or ornamental, whereas those of the flatterer, being by their own nature diseased, require the assistance of many remedies, and those exquisite in their kind And hence in accidental meetings true friends will often pass by each other without opening their lips, but give and receive their mutual tokens of inward love and affection by a look only or a smile *, but the flatterer runs up eagerly to meet or overtake you, greets you afar off, and, if perchance you should first accost him, apologizes for his seeming inattention with the most solemn asseverations, and appeals to witnesses that he never saw you Thus too in a variety of actions the real friend omits many trifling and minute circumstances, neither accurately perform-

---

* Δι τοῦ, φιλοῦντας ὄψιν, ου λόγους, ἔχειν.
It is not words that constitute the friend.

ing nor officiously investigating every thing, nor intruding himself into every service, but the parasite in all matters of this sort is constant and indefatigable in his zeal and industry, and will not give another either the time or opportunity of serving you, but is eager to receive your commands, and, if he receive them not, takes it much at heart, or rather is totally dispirited, and complains bitterly of his fate. These then are plain and evident marks to those who have sense, not of genuine and virtuous friendship, but of that false and meretricious sort which obtrudes too fervently its embraces.

But it may not be amiss to observe first the difference between the true and the false friend with respect to the nature of their promises and engagements, for it was well said by those before us, that the true friend makes no other promise than this,

If it be possible and in my power,

But the false one cries out,

Speak your request and deem your will obey'd *;

And hence the comedians introduce such men as these,

Let me but see that Soldier face to face,
If I don't bruise him to a pumpion,
And make him soft as spunge—.

* Pope Il. xiv. 224.

Moreover, no true friend will become a co-adjutor in any undertaking, if he be not first consulted thereon, and shall have approved both of its propriety and utility: but the flatterer, even though you should request him to examine the business and deliver his opinion upon it, readily yields to your desires and even spurs them on, not only through a willingness to comply with and gratify your wishes, but through fear lest you should suspect him of being averse to the cause. For you cannot easily find any rich or great man who will say,

> Let him a beggar be, or, if you please,
> Much worse than beggar, who doth wish me well,
> And boldly speaks the language of his heart

For they like the tragedians, have need of a chorus of friends who will join in concert with them, or else the applauses of a theatre. And hence Merope, in the tragedy, gives this exhortation,

> Choose for your friends those men who never fawn,
> Nor flatter in their words; but let your doors
> Be barr'd against the wretch, who strives to gain
> Your favour by base actions, and subserves your will.

But the rich instead of following this advice, act quite the contrary; for such men as will not fawn and flatter, but will often oppose them for the best, are despised, and precluded from their presence while they who will not hesitate to do any thing base and illiberal, and practise any imposture in order to ingratiate themselves, are admitted not only within their doors and habitations, but even into their affections and most secret concerns. Some indeed of these flatterers less artful than others, neither think it their duty, nor deem themselves worthy to give their advice upon such serious occasions, but are desirous only of being employed in the inferior capacity of agents. but others more subtile enter into your counsels and deliberations, if such we may call that hesitating look, that contraction of the brow, and that shrewd nod of the head, which they so frequently make use of, for they speak not a word, unless perchance when you deliver your opinion, the flatterer then cries out, " By " Hercules you have just got the start of me, for " I was going to make the same observation." And as mathematicians say that superficies and lines are neither curved nor extended nor moved by themselves, since they exist only in the mind, and are without substance, but are curved, extended, and change their situation in conjunction with the bodies whose extremities they are, so you will always find the flatterer closely following the words, the opinions, the senses, and passions of another. And therefore in all matters of this sort the disparity between him and the friend is easily discernible.

Nor is it less easy to discover him in his manner of performing any service: for the kind offices of a friend, like the chief powers of a brute-animal, lie deep, concealed from view, without any external pomp or parade: and as a physician is often of the greatest service to his patient when he least expects it, so the friend whether in your presence or absence, is wont to confer the greatest benefits upon you, and have your good most at heart when perhaps you are least aware of it. Such was Arcesilaus, in many other instances indeed, but especially when he visited Apelles the Chian, who lay sick in bed, for being made acquainted with his poverty, he returned again soon after, bringing with him twenty drachms [46], and placing himself near his bed-side, "You have " nothing here, said he, but the elements of " Empedocles,

" Fire, water, earth, and the surrounding air,

" nor indeed do you lie comfortably," and at the same time moving his pillow, secretly put the money under it, which when the old nurse afterwards found, and full of admiration told Apelles of it, "This, said the sick man with a smile, is " Arcesilaus's trick." And truly children resemble their parents in philosophy [47]. For when Cephisocrates lay under an accusation for some public offence, Lacydes (the disciple of Arcesilaus) stood near him upon his trial with many other of his friends, and when, upon his ring's being demanded by his accuser, he let it drop softly upon the ground through the folds of his garment, Lacydes, seeing what he had done, put his foot upon it and concealed it now the proof of Cephisocrates's guilt lay in this ring, and after his acquittal upon his paying his respects to the judges, one of them, who it seems had seen through the whole transaction, ordered him to return his thanks to Lacydes, and immediately related the whole story though Lacydes had mentioned it to no one [48].

Thus am I persuaded that the Gods are often our benefactors when we are not sensible of their goodness, and this too upon no other principle than the pleasure which they take in acts of kindness and benevolence

But the actions of the flatterer can boast neither of their justice, nor sincerity, nor simplicity, nor candour, but are attended with that noise and bustle, and sweat, and that contraction of the brow, which bears the appearance, and raises an opinion of much toil and zeal in your service like an over-laboured painting which by its gawdy colours, the broken folds in the vestment, and its various wrinkles and angles, attracts to itself the semblance of much accuracy and perspicuity.

The flatterer is also very disgusting and tedious in recounting the number of journeys that he has undertaken, and the cares and anxieties which he hath undergone for your sake, whether it be that he is relating to you the many friends whom he was compelled to disoblige, or the various sufferings that he hath experienced, insomuch that you may say " The business was not worth such great " pains." For every instance of favour with which a man is upbraided, becomes irksome, odious, and intolerable. But as to flatterers, at the very moment that they are conferring a favour, without waiting to see its effect upon you, they accompany it with reproaches for your want of gratitude[49]. Whereas the friend, even though it should be necessary to speak of any particular service, mentions the subject in a very delicate manner and says not a word of himself. Thus the Lacedæmonians, having supplied the inhabitants of Smyrna with some corn in a time of scarcity, and upon their being struck with admiration at the greatness of the favour, said, " that it was " no such great matter, for we have only passed " a decree to deprive ourselves and cattle of one " day's dinner." For a kindness thus bestowed is not only generous and liberal, but more acceptable to the receivers, because they believe that it does not greatly distress the giver.

But it is not so much from the tedious, disgustful narrative of his performances, nor from the facility and readiness of his promises, that we may best discover the nature of the flatterer, but rather from observing how far he obeys or disobeys the rule of virtue in his services, and how far he differs from the friend in the pleasure or utility attending them. For a real friend will not, as Gorgias declared, require from the hands of his familiar and intimate those things only which are just, while he himself will not hesitate to do for the other's sake many which are unjust,

> For virtue's paths he only will pursue,
> Nor in the road of vice will bear him company,

rather indeed he will turn him aside from such actions as are likely to reflect disgrace upon him, and if he cannot persuade him will well apply the reproof of Phocion to Antipater, "You cannot use me both as a friend and flatterer," that is, both as a friend and not a friend. For it is our duty to share with our friend in good actions but not in bad, to assist him with our counsel but not for fraudulent purposes, with our testimony but not in practising deceit, and in short to partake of his misfortunes but not in his injustice. for as it is not eligible for a friend even to be conscious of the moral turpitude of another, how much less is it to be his associate in actions which reflect shame and disgrace? Thus when the Spartans were defeated by Antipater, and were entering upon articles of peace, they required him to impose upon them any conditions he pleased however severe, provided there was nothing dishonourable in them. thus too does the friend, if any service occur that is attended with trouble, danger, or expence, he is the first that demands to be called out, and cheerfully to partake of it, but where there is any mixture of dishonour there alone he will refuse compliance and beg you to excuse him But it is quite the contrary with the flatterer, in all laborious and dangerous enterprizes he refuses his assistance, and if, like an earthen vessel, you ring him upon trial [51], he sounds crackt and hollow, and has always in his mouth some frivolous and illiberal excuses; whereas in any mean, ignoble, or disgraceful office, abuse him and trample upon him as much as ever you please, he puts up with every insult and thinks nothing a reproach. Consider the ape, it can neither guard your house like a dog, nor bear burthen as a horse, nor plough the ground like an ox, but sustains every species of scurrility and abuse, and makes itself the instrument of ridicule. Thus the flatterer, since he is unable to reason with you, to share in your expences, or participate in your contests and dangers, and since he fails in every serious pursuit and laborious undertaking, very cheerfully offers his service in all clandestine enterprizes, a faithful minister of your pleasures and pander to your lust, very diligent in clearing up the account of the expences of a debauch, and by no means remiss in the preparation of a dinner, and moreover very attentive and obsequious to your mistress, whereas if he be desired to behave with harshness or severity towards your relations, and to assist in repudiating your wife, he obeys without feeling either remorse or sympathy. So that neither in this respect is it difficult to discover him, for lay any injunctions upon him that you please however ignominious or dishonourable, he is very ready to give up himself in order to gratify you.

But one may gain no small information of his character by observing how he stands affected towards your other intimates, wherein he differs widely from the real and true friend, for the greatest pleasure which the latter can receive is to share and return your love among many others, and this object he will always strive to obtain for you, that you may have many friends whom you respect and are respected by [52] for being of opinion that every thing is common among friends, so he thinks that nothing should be more common than friends themselves. But the false, spurious counterfeit, inasmuch as he is conscious of the injury that he does true amity, which he holds in the same light as a base coin, is indeed naturally invidious and shews his envy towards those of the same stamp as himself, endeavouring to outdo them in buffoonery and loquacity, but with respect to his betters, these he fears and reverences, not indeed running on foot with a Lydian chariot, but, in the words of Simonides, unable even to produce mere lead against refined gold.

Since therefore he is sure to be found of a light, factitious, and deceitful nature, when brought under examination against true, weighty, and solid friendship, having no plea or excuse to make, but being fully convicted, he imitates the conduct of a certain painter who had drawn a cock extremely ill, for as the one order'd his servant to drive the original as far off as possible from his picture, so the other would drive off all real friends and not suffer them to approach, and if he cannot do this, he openly indeed courts, and flatters, and reverences them as his superiors, while secretly he sows the seeds of calumny and slander, and where clandestine malice has once raised a wound, though it does not immediately answer all the purposes the flatterer intended, yet he remembers well the advice of Medius. Now this Medius was, as it were, the leader of the band of parasites around Alexander, and marshalled as the chief foe to virtue and reputation this man used to exhort his followers boldly to attack and vilify the characters of others, telling them, " that though the object of " their slander might heal its wound, the scar " would remain [53]."

It was by such scars, or rather gangrenes and cancers that Alexander was almost eaten up, and caused his best friends Callisthenes, Parmenio, and

Philotas to be put to death, while he himself fell an easy prey to the Agnones, Bagoæ, Agesiæ, and Demetrii who worshipped and decorated him like a barbarian idol. So great a charm is flattery, and the greatest, as it seems, where men are thought of the greatest consequence, for the high opinion which they entertain of their own virtues, and the desire of the same opinion being entertained by others, give courage to the flatterer and credit to his impostures. For though the more lofty and elevated any place is, the more inaccessible is it to the besiegers, yet that pride and elevation of a mind that is puffed up and debilitated either by prosperity, or greatness of birth and family, affords an easy approach even to the meanest aggressor.

Wherefore we now repeat the exhortation that we gave in the beginning of this treatise, to strip ourselves of every vain opinion of our own merits, for self-love being the first to flatter us within, makes us more easy of access to external flattery, inasmuch as we are already prepared for its reception. But if, acting in obedience to the divine command, and studying to *know ourselves*, (as a precept of the utmost importance to every man) we examine our own nature, education, and manners, and consider how many failings, errors, and vices are blended in our words, in our actions, in our affections, we shall not so readily yield ourselves up to be insulted and trod upon by sycophants. Alexander indeed used to say that he discredited those who ranked him among the Gods, chiefly by reason of his indulging in sleep and in the use of women, as he was more addicted to these failings than became his dignity so we, having ever in view our own manifold vices, afflictions, infirmities and errors, shall find that we stand not so much in need of a friend to praise and applaud our virtues, as one who will freely chide and reprove us for our faults [54] For how few are there who have the courage to admonish their friends, and even among these few how rare is it to find any who are capable of doing it with judgement, the generality of those who have the fidelity to interpose their advice upon such occasions, being apt to mistake rude reprehension and severe invective for an honest and laudable freedom*.

But surely it is with admonition as with any other remedy, if it be misapplied it serves only to create a great deal of useless trouble and affliction, and in some measure produces the same effect with pain, which flattery does with pleasure For our morals are not only injured by unseasonable commendation, but also by unseasonable rebuke, and it is this which chiefly forces men into the hands of the flatterer, pouring down, as it were, like water from the steep opposed precipice of censure, into the smooth level vale of adulation Wherefore we

---

* The latter part of this sentence is translated by the elegant Mr Melmoth See his Lælius, p 126 Note (b)

ought to temper our reproof with moderation, and apply such a portion of candour and prudence as may take from it all violence and severity[55], just as we would remove from the eye too powerful a ray of light, that thus our friends may not be compelled to fly to the shade and retreat of the flatterer, in order to avoid that pain and uneasiness which they suffer from men who are perpetually blaming and finding fault with every thing. For all vicious habits, my Philopappus, are to be corrected by means of virtue, not by the opposite vices, as some men falsely imagine, who think, that bashfulness is to be avoided by impudence, and rusticity of manners by buffoonery, and that they are as far removed as possible from the imputation of effeminacy and cowardice, if they are approximate to impudence and audacity. Others again defend themselves against the charge of superstition, by atheism; against folly, by cunning and knavery, turning and twisting their manners, like a bended rod, from one extreme to the other, through ignorance of the straight line.

But it is a most ignominious mode of avoiding the appearance of flattery, to be offensive without any useful purposes, and by the odious unpleasantness of a demeanour wholly rustic and destitute of every art that conciliates good will, to shun what is illiberal and low in friendship, as if we regarded the coarse ribaldry of comick dialogue as the true enjoyment of free conversation.

Since therefore, on the one hand, it is disgraceful for us, in our endeavours to oblige our friend, to fall into adulation, so on the other, does it equally misbecome us, in striving to escape the imputation of flattery, to destroy friendship itself and all that tender anxiety which accompanies it, by giving too great a loose to our reproof and censure but we ought to avoid both extremes, and as in all other things, so in freedom of admonition, the true measure of right and wrong is to be taken from the middle line[50]. The nature of the argument seems to require me to close my treatise with some observations upon this subject

Since then we plainly see that this freedom in reprimanding others is liable to so many objections, let us in the first place very carefully strip it of every particle of self-interest, that our censures and reproofs may not have the appearance of originating from any private injury of our own, for the generality of men think that every thing which is said for our own sakes does not arise from benevolence, but from passion, and is no longer admonition, but complaint, for free and open reproof is friendly and venerable, but complaint savours much of selfishness and illiberality. And hence it is that we reverence and admire those men who admonish us with freedom and sincerity, whilst we despise those who are full of complaints, and retaliate their accusations. Thus Agamemnon could not bear the reproofs of Achilles though they seemed given with moderation, but submitted with the greatest patience to these severe reprimands of Ulysses,

> What shameful words, unkingly as thou art,
> Fall from that trembling tongue and tim'rous heart?
> O were thy sway the curse of meaner pow'rs,
> And thou the shame of any host but ours*!

These I say he submitted to with patience, being convinced of the salutary wisdom and prudence with which they were delivered: for the one in reprimanding him gratified no private resentment, but spoke his sentiments freely for the welfare of Greece, whereas the censures of the other seemed merely the effect of revenge and passion. And yet this very Achilles, though by no means of a mild and lenient disposition, but fierce and inexorable,

> And prompt e'en him that's innocent to blame,

patiently suffered his friend Patroclus to handle him in the following severe manner

> O man unpitying! if of man thy race,
> But sure thou spring'st not from a soft embrace,

* Pope Il. xiv. 90.

Nor ever am'rous hero caus'd thy birth,
Nor ever tender Goddess brought thee forth
Some rugged rock's hard entrails gave thee form,
And raging seas produc'd thee in a storm,
A soul well suiting that tempestuous kind,
So rough thy manners, so untam'd thy mind *.

For as Hyperides the orator desired the Athenians to consider not only whether he were severe in his animadversions, but whether his severity were disinterested, so the admonition of the friend, being free from every selfish affection, strikes us with awe and reverence and moreover, if it appear manifest that our friend, in the midst of his reproof, purposely avoids mentioning any injuries done to himself, but censures and severely reprimands us for those faults wherein himself is unconcerned, the force of such a reproof as this is irresistible, and the bitterness and severity of the admonition are increased by the amiable sweetness of the admonisher And hence it is wisely said that in all disputes and differences with our friends we ought so to conduct ourselves as not to be inattentive to their honour and interest [57].

Nor is it less a mark of friendship, when a man, who seems to be neglected and despised himself, shall freely chide and admonish his friend for the neglect with which he treats others Thus Plato, at a time when he was at variance with,

* Pope II. xvi 46

and hated by Dionysius, begged the favour of an interview, which Dionysius granted in expectation of hearing an account of his complaints and grievances, but the Philosopher thus addressed him: "If you should hear, Dionysius, that any evil-minded person had come to Sicily, with an intention of doing you some injury, but was frustrated for want of an opportunity, would you suffer him to leave the island with impunity?" "Far from it, replied Dionysius, for we ought, Plato, to detest and punish not only the bad actions of our enemies, but also their malicious intentions." "If then, returned Plato, any one should come here impressed with the most benevolent sentiments towards you, and desirous of rendering you some service, but you do not give him the opportunity, is it right to dismiss him with ingratitude and contempt?" And Dionysius asking him, who that man was, "Æschines, replied Plato, a man of as amiable manners as any among the companions of Socrates, and well qualified by his superior abilities to instruct and edify those with whom he is conversant, yet although he has made a long voyage in order to enjoy your conversation on philosophical subjects, is neglected by you and despised." This behaviour so affected Dionysius, that he instantly threw his hands round Plato, and cordially embraced him, admiring the benevolence of his disposition, and the greatness of his soul, and at the same time paid great attention to Æschines, and treated him with respect.

In the second place, let us purify our reprehensions of every unpalatable seasoning, and banish from them all expressions of reproach, scorn, ridicule, and scurrility. For as a surgeon ought to be very attentive to preserve neatness in his operations, and as every kind of unsteady, wavering, superfluous motion should be far removed from his hand, so freedom of reproof, provided its respectability be preserved, admits of a proper degree of humour and urbanity, but on the approach of the least impudent, scurrilous, or opprobrious language, all its purposes are defeated. And therefore the musician very shrewdly and pertinently silenced Philip, who was beginning to dispute with him about notes and sounds, by telling him, " God forbid, O King! that you should " ever be so unfortunate as to know these things " better than I do." But Epicharmus, the Pythagorean philosopher, acted very imprudently, when, upon being invited by Hiero to a dinner a few days after he had put to death several of his companions, he replied, " But you did not invite " your friends to your late sacrifice." Nor was the response of Antipho at all better judged, when, the discourse turning upon the best sort of brass, and Dionysius inquiring which it was, he told him, " That, with which the Athenians made the " statues of Harmodius and Aristogiton [55]." For neither is this bitterness and severity of any service, nor are these scurrilous jests at all agreeable, but such language bears rather the appearance of intemperance and animosity blended with contumely and malice, and they who indulge in it often bring on their own ruin, plainly dancing, according to the proverb, on the brink of a well. Thus Antipho was put to death by Dionysius. And Timagenes lost the friendship of Augustus Cæsar, not for the freedom of his reproofs, but because he would scatter his abuse and slander in the public walks and convivial meetings for no serious purpose,

But to excite the laughter of the Greeks,

alledging the cause of friendship as a pretext for calumny. Thus too our comick writers often introduce upon the stage many grave and salutary remarks, but the ridicule and buffoonery which are mixed with them, like bad seasoning with a good dish, vitiate the whole and render the admonition useless and insignificant, so that the speakers acquire only the reputation of being scurrilous and abusive, and the audience derive no advantage from what is said. At other times indeed we should relax in our severity, and indulge with our friends in the cheerful jest and laugh, but in our admonition and censures we should carefully observe a proper degree of gravity and decorum, and if the subject be of more serious importance, our passions, gestures and tone of voice should be so regulated as to give weight and energy to our sentiments.

But we ought to be very careful that our reproofs be well timed, for a neglect of opportunity, which does so much injury in all other things, is particularly destructive to the advantages of free admonition. It appears indeed sufficiently manifest that we should avoid all manner of censure amid the pleasures of the table and the glass, for that man tends only to cast a cloud over a clear sky, who awakens, amid the mirth and good humour of the company, any discourse which knits the brow and contracts the countenance, as if it were in direct opposition to the Lysian God[59], who, according to Pindar,

> Loosens the bands of care.

Moreover, such unseasonable reproof is attended with no small danger, for the minds of men when elevated by wine are prone to passion, and inebriety often converts the admonition received into hatred and animosity and in short it is neither generous nor manly, but shews a timid disposition in a man who dares not deliver his sentiments in the moments of sobriety, but like a cowardly dog barks and growls at the table. There is no occasion therefore for me to dwell any longer upon this subject.

But since there are many persons who neither dare, nor think it right to admonish and correct their friends, while favoured by the smile of fortune, imagining that prosperity has set them above the reach of admonition, but who will insult and trample upon them, when fallen from their grandeur and humbled by misfortune, and will pour forth their censures upon them, like a river that has overflown its banks, taking a malicious pleasure in their depression, on account of their former superiority to themselves Since I say there are several persons of this description, it may not be unadviseable to discuss this matter, and answer that question of Euripides,

> When fate and fortune smile, what need of friends?

Since they who are in prosperity have the greatest need of friends to admonish and direct them, and to depress that pride and haughtiness which are the usual attendants upon wealth[60], for few are there whose prosperity is accompanied by wisdom Therefore most men stand in need of that foreign, adventitious aid and counsel which may restrain them, too much puffed up and agitated by fortune, but when adverse fate shall have humbled their pride and stript them of their grandeur, their misfortunes are alone sufficient to admonish them of past errors, and instil sorrow and repentance. Surely then in the affliction that attends adversity there can be no occasion for harsh admonition, nor severe reproof, but after such a change it is truly delightful to meet with that consolation which raises the depressed spirits,

<blockquote>In Friendship's soothing eye</blockquote>

Thus Xenophon observes that the mild and benevolent aspect of Clearchus in the heat of battle and in the midst of difficulties, gave new life and confidence to the soldiery. Whereas the man who applies any censure or reproof to one labouring under misfortunes, like an acute medicine to a diseased and inflamed eye, neither performs a cure, nor alleviates his pain, but adds anger only to his sorrows, and exasperates his affliction. A man in health indeed very quietly submits to the remonstrances of his friend, whether he reprove his too free use of wine and women, or find fault with his sloth, his idleness, his frequent bathing, or unseasonable gluttony but to a sick man it is intolerable, and even more grievous than the disease itself, to be told that, " all your " evils have been caused by your own intem- " perance, voluptuousness, luxurious eating, and " debauchery." " O what unseasonableness, O " man! I am writing my will, and castor and " scammony are prescribed me by the physicians, " and do you admonish and philosophize?"

Thus then the situation of the unfortunate stands more in need of our lenity and consolation, than it requires any severe or sententious reproof for even nurses when their children fall do not run up to scold them, but raise them from the ground, wash them clean, and restore them again to order, and then perhaps reprimand and chastise them

It is reported of Demetrius Phalereus that, after his banishment from his country when he was living at Thebes in an obscure and mean condition, he was very uneasy at seeing the Philosopher Crates approaching towards him, expecting nothing from him but the harsh treatment of a Cynic but when Crates mildly accosted him, and entered into a discourse upon banishment as if there was nothing so grievous in it, as to make him unhappy or miserable, but rather that it liberated him from the danger and uncertainty attending public affairs, and at the same time exhorted him to confide in his own greatness and constancy of mind, the poor man instantly became more placid, and. encouraged by what he heard, said to his friends around him, " Cursed " be all those employments and occupations by " which I have been deprived of the knowledge " of such a man as this."

> For to th' afflicted, words of comfort give,
> But with the headstrong fool use sharp rebuke.

These then are the manners which are adopted by generous and noble minds But the mean and illiberal flatterers of your prosperity, as Demosthenes remarks of ruptures and spasms which are then most affected when any misfortune befalls the body, so I say these men upon any change in your fortune acquire fresh vigour, as if they were pleased with, and enjoyed your adversity and indeed if there be any circumstance wanting to remind you that you fell by your own imprudent and rash counsel, the following lines of the Poet are sufficient for the purpose,

> 'Twas not with my consent, for much and oft
> Have I dissuaded you.

Where then is it allowable for a man to be severe with his friend, and when may he exert the force of free admonition? Whenever he may be invited by an opportunity to repress the inordinate career of pleasure, anger, or contumely, or to allay the thirst of gold, or to oppose himself to any other rash and foolish passion. Thus Solon freely admonished Croesus, whom the instability of fortune had corrupted and puffed up, telling him *to regard the end* Thus too Socrates humbled the pride of Alcibiades, and forced him by his arguments into unfeigned tears, and turned his heart Such were the remonstrances of Cyrus to Cyaxeres, and thus dealt Plato with Dion, exhorting him, at a time when he shone in his greatest glory, and had fixt all mens eyes upon him by the magnificence and beauty of his exploits, to guard against pride and arrogance, as being the companions of solitude [61] Speusippus too wrote to him, not to be elevated by the little applauses of women and children, but to take care to increase the glory and renown of the academy, by adorning Sicily with his sanctity and justice, and his wholesome and excellent laws. Thus did not Euctus and Eulæus, the companions and favourites of Perseus, for as long as Perseus was in prosperity they were ever flattering and fawning upon him, and like the other sycophants very obsequiously attended him, but after the battle of Pydna, wherein he was defeated by the Romans and betook himself to flight, they inveighed bitterly against him and reproached him with his several errors and offences, until that the poor man, tortured by grief and rage, put them both to the sword. Let this explanation suffice respecting opportunities in general.

But those which our friends themselves often present to us, should by no means be overlooked, but rather readily laid hold of, by him who has their interest at heart; for sometimes a question, or a narrative, or some praise or censure of similar actions or pursuits in others, is as it were a prelude to an honest and open freedom. Thus we are told that Demaratus came from Corinth to Macedon at the time that Philip was at variance with his wife and son; and upon Philip's embracing him, and asking him, " how the Greeks kept

" up their harmony?" Demaratus, who was his familiar friend, replied, " Truly, O Philip, it be-
" comes you to inquire about the concord of the
" Athenians and Peloponnesians, while you over-
" look your own house labouring under such dis-
" cord and animosity." That also was a good answer of Diogenes the Cynic, who, coming into the camp of Philip at the time that he was preparing to march to battle against the Greeks, was seized and carried into his presence, and the king not knowing him asked whether he were a spy?
" Yes truly, O Philip, said he, I am a spy over
" your rashness and folly, by which without the
" least necessity you are going in one hour to
" submit your life and kingdom to the hazard
" of a die." Though this perhaps may be thought too severe

But there is another opportunity no less favourable to admonition, and that is, when our friend is already humbled to a sense of his errors by the reproaches which he has received from others, and this opportunity a man of a liberal mind will diligently use in repelling and silencing his accusers, while he himself will privately reprimand his friend and admonish him to be more circumspect in his conduct, tho' it be upon no other account but to avoid giving his enemies a handle for abuse " For how can these men open their
" mouths, or where can they find any thing to say

" against you, if you banish all those failings
" which now expose you to their censure[62]." By
such behaviour as this all the sorrow and vexation
fall to the lot of the accuser, and the advantages
derived are attributed to him who gave the admonition. But there are some who chide still
more gracefully, for they will censure and reprimand in others those faults which they know that
their friends are guilty of, and by these means convert them to the path of rectitude. Thus our master and preceptor Ammonius, perceiving once at
an evening-lecture that some of his scholars had
dined too luxuriously for the simple manner of
the Greeks[63], ordered the freedman to stripe his
own son, alledging that he cannot dine without
vinegar, and at the same time cast a look towards
us, so that every one who was guilty sensibly felt
the rebuke.

Moreover, we should be very cautious how we
reprove our friend in the company of others, remembering the story of Plato. For Socrates
having once in a dispute at table rebuked one of
his companions rather too severely, " Would it
" not have been better, said Plato, to have
" spoken these things in private?" " And you
" too, replied Socrates, would not you have
" done better, if you had said this to me in pri-
" vate?" And Pythagoras having treated a disciple of his with too much severity before others,
it is said that the youth hanged himself, and Py-

thagoras from that time never again admonished another in the presence of a third person. For the reproof and manifestation of vice, as of an unbecoming disease, ought to be made as secret as possible, and not exhibited with the pomp and ostentation of a public spectacle, nor exposed before witnesses and spectators [64] for it is not so much a mark of friendship, as of sophistry, for a man ostentatiously to recommend himself to the company, and to acquire his own reputation from the failings of another, like the surgeons who exhibit their operations upon the theatres in order to obtain practice. But without any reproach on our part, which should never be united with wholesome and salutary admonition, vice may of itself be considered of an obstinate and stubborn nature, for it is not love only which, according to Euripides,

Persists the more, the more it be reprov'd,

but every other passion and imperfection, which, if a man censure before others and with severity, he will be so far from curing, that he will absolutely banish every remnant of shame and modesty. As therefore Plato recommends those elders who would instil reverence into the breast of youth, first to set the example themselves and revere the young, so a modest reproof of a friend has the most powerful effect in awakening a sense of shame in the person reproved, and a cautious, gradual attack upon the offender undermines and destroys that vice which is already covered with confusion. And therefore according to the excellent rule of the old Bard,

>In whispers breathe the fondness of thy heart*.

But it is in the highest degree improper to reveal the faults of a husband in the hearing of his wife, a parent in the sight of his children, a lover in the presence of his beloved, or a teacher before his scholars, for men are almost distracted with grief and rage when they are rebuked in the presence of those from whom they expect reverence and esteem. And I verily believe that Alexander was not so much irritated at the rebuke of Clitus on account of the wine that he had drunk, as because it seemed to lessen him in the eyes of his companions. And Aristomenes, the tutor of Ptolemy Epiphanes, laid himself open to parasites and flatterers for once waking the king out of a nap into which he had fallen in the presence of a foreign embassy, for these sycophants pretended to be much enraged at the insult offered to his Majesty, saying, "If after so much vigi‑ lance and fatigue you should happen to be overpower'd by sleep, we ought privately to admonish you of it and not lay our hands upon you before so many witnesses" this so operated

* Pope Odyss xvii 675.

upon the king that he sent the poor man a cup of poison and compelled him to drink it off. And Aristophanes accusing Cleon of the same fault says that

While strangers hear, he vilifies the state,

and thereby irritates and inflames the minds of the Athenians. Wherefore in censuring our friend we ought carefully to avoid all appearance of ostentation, or of courting popular applause, and our admonition should solely be directed to his interest and welfare.

And indeed what Thucydides has made the Corinthians say of themselves, that they are well qualified to animadvert upon the failings of others, is certainly a just remark, and ought to be had in remembrance by every man who takes upon him to reprove his neighbour. For as Lysander told a Megarensian, who was boldly haranguing among the allies for the liberties of Greece, " that his " words had need of a city." so freedom in reprehension requires to be recommended by the probity of the person who applies it, and this is most true of those who admonish and correct others. It is therefore for this reason that Plato used to say that he admonished Speusippus by his very way of life. Thus too Xenocrates seeing once the dissolute Polemo enter his school, and casting only his eyes upon him, brought him to a compleat sense of his folly and turned him from the paths of vice[65]. But when a man of light and vicious morals is too free in his censures upon others, let him hear the Bard,

> Others diseases he essays to heal,
> Himself all over sores

But because it may often happen that the vicious and debauched in their intercourse with others of the same stamp, may be led by circumstances to admonish and correct them, the most gentle and courteous manner of doing it would be, somehow or other to enclose and involve themselves in the same guilt. In which sense it is said by the Poet,

> Why stand we deedless here, great Tydeus' son,
> And why forget we all our ancient worth *!

And again,

> But now we dare not meet the single arm,
> Of the brave Hector.

And thus Socrates used insensibly to reprove the young men for their ignorance, by professing that he was ignorant himself, and that he ought to accompany them in the study of virtue and search after truth. For they indeed who appear to labour under the same infirmities, and to be correcting and reforming themselves at the same

---

* The Reader may compare Pope Il. xi. 408 a few of whose words I have borrowed

time that they correct their friends, not only conciliate their good will but give weight and authority to their own admonitions. But he who magnifies himself in detracting from another, as if he were quite free from every human imperfection, unless indeed his great age claim our respect, or his glory and reputation be well established in the world, is only grievous and irksome, and never of any service. And therefore Phoenix, that he might not seem to admonish Achilles as if he himself were free from passion and without error, very properly brought his own faults into view, having once in a fit of passion taken up the resolution of killing his father, and quickly checking his rashness,

> T' escape the impious name of Parricide.

For such behaviour as this penetrates deeply into the hearts of men, and we obey more readily those who seem to have similar infirmities with ourselves, than those who appear to hold us in contempt.

But since an inflamed eye cannot bear the approach of any glare of light, nor a mind that is agitated by passion admit of reproof and admonition untempered with corrective, one of the best remedies will be to qualify our censures with a slight mixture of praise, as in the following,

> Think and subdue! on dastards dead to fame
> I waste no anger, for they feel no shame

> But you, the pride, the flow'r of all our host,
> My heart weeps blood to see your glory lost *!

And again,

> Where, Pandarus, are all thy honours now,
> Thy winged arrows, and unerring bow,
> Thy matchless skill, thy yet unrivall'd fame,
> And boasted glory of the Lycian name †.

And such expressions too as the following very manifestly recall them who have been led astray,

> Where now is Œdipus and those far-fam'd Ænigmas?

And in another place,

> Does the much suff'ring Hercules speak thus?

For by such means we not only relax the imperious harshness and severity of censure, but create in the person reproved an emulation of himself, inasmuch as he becomes ashamed of his present vices by being reminded of his former virtues, and is obliged to propose his own laudable actions an example for his future imitation. But if, in order to reform the vicious man, we compare him with others, such as his equals, or fellow citizens, or relations, we only enrage and and exasperate the stubborn obstinacy of vice, and he is apt to exclaim in a passion, "why

* Pope Il. xiii. 157.   † Pope Il. v. 28.

"don't you go then to my betters, and not "pester me in this manner?" When therefore we admonish our friends we ought very carefully to avoid praising others, unless indeed it be their parents thus Agamemnon chides Diomed,

> Surely the warrior Tydeus has begot
> A son, degenerate from his noble blood.

Thus too Ulysses, in the Tragedy inscribed Scyriæ, reprimanded Achilles,

> How can the son of Peleus here obscure,
> Effeminate, his glorious ancestry,
> Born of a Sire, the best of all the Greeks

But above all the person who is reproved should beware of retorting the reproof, and opposing censure to censure, for it quickly lights up and creates dissention, and indeed such a conduct would have less the appearance of retaliation, than impatience under reproof.[66] It is more adviseable therefore to bear with the remonstrances of our friend, for if he himself shall afterwards commit any fault that is worthy of reprehension, this very behaviour of ours in some measure gives boldness and authority to our words. for being reminded, without the least mention of any past offence, that he himself is not wont to overlook the errors of his friends, but to reprimand and admonish them, he will more readily receive the correction, as being rather the return of kindness and benevolence, than of anger or resentment.

Moreover as Thucydides has remarked that he is well advised who subjects himself to envy on account of the greatness of his exploits, so it becomes the friend to take upon himself the ungrateful office of censor only upon weighty and important matters: but if he take umbrage upon every trivial occasion and at every person, and treat his familiars more like a pedagogue than a friend, his advice in more serious concerns will be feeble and ineffectual, like a physician who abuses any sharp and powerful medicine, (precious indeed and necessary at other times) by prescribing it for every slight and trifling disease. He will therefore carefully guard against too great a frequency of complaint, and if his friend should be of that cavilling, captious disposition which animadverts upon every trifle, he will then have a handle for attacking his greater offences. Thus Philotimus the physician, upon a patient of his who had an abscess at his liver shewing him his sore finger, " you have nothing to do my friend, says he, " with the roots of your nails." In like manner when we hear a man chiding another for some trivial and insignificant failing, we have a fair opportunity of saying, " why do we talk of this " man's jokes, or jests, or his bottle? let him, " my friend, cast off his mistress, and throw " away his dice, and in other respects we have

' reason to commend him." For he who is pardoned for his lesser offences, very readily gives his friend the liberty of animadverting upon his greater but the man who is perpetually scolding, and at all times of a sour and morose temper, who knows every thing, and is always inquisitive and meddling, is not only insufferable to his children, or brethren, but cannot even be endured by his servants.

But as Euripides remarks of old age that it has some good blended with its evil[67], so also have the infirmities and follies of our friends, we ought therefore not only to observe their failings but also their virtues, and in truth to shew ourselves ready to praise the one before we blame the other for as iron which has been softened by the force of heat, receives a density and hardness from the application of cold, so the friend, relaxed and warmed by praise, admits with greater readiness the temper, as it were, of reproof. we have then an opportunity of remonstrating with him, "Are
" those actions worthy to be compared with these?
" Do you see the fruit which virtue yields to those
" who cultivate her? These are what we your
" friends require of you, these properly belong to
" you, to these you were formed by nature, but
" with respect to those other pursuits, banish them
" far from you,

" Or to the mountain-top, or whelming deep."

For as an humane physician would wish rather by sleep and diet to heal the malady of his patient, than by castor and scammony, so the kind and benevolent friend, the good father, and tender master take less delight in reforming the morals of another by censure than by praise. For there is nothing which takes away so much the harshness from our reproof, and increases its advantages, as to be sparing of our anger and to address the delinquent with lenity and benevolence. And therefore we ought not to press too severely upon him when he disavows any particular act, nor restrain him from justifying himself, but rather to help him out in some plausible pretext, and if he shun the more dishonourable excuse, to shew ourselves more favourably inclined towards him. Thus Hector chides his brother Paris,

 Thy hate to Troy is this the time to shew *

As if his retreat from the battle were neither flight nor cowardice, but the effect of anger and resentment. And thus Nestor tells Agamemnon.

 But you obey'd the greatness of your soul

For it is in my opinion more courteous and obliging to say that you did such a thing through ignorance or inadvertency, than you have acted unjustly and dishonourably, and do not contend

* Pope Il. vi. 456.

with your brother, is a more civil expression than don't envy him, and it is kinder to say, fly this woman who debauches you, than leave off debauching her. For that reproof which is intended to heal the infirmities that our friends already labour under requires to be applied in the manner I have stated, but a contrary mode is to be adopted, when we wish to prevent the contracting of them for whenever it shall be found necessary to deter our friends from the commission of any crime, or to oppose any violent and headstrong passion, or to incite and spur on those to honourable pursuits who are of a languid and sluggish humour, we ought then to ascribe their failings to some unbecoming and dishonourable cause Thus Ulysses, in one of the tragedies of Sophocles, when stimulating the courage of Achilles, tells him that he was not indignant on account of the supper,

> But now thou tremblest seeing the walls of Troy,

And upon Achilles being exceedingly enraged at this and declaring that he would return with his fleet,

> I know what 'tis you shun, not my reproach,
> But Hector's near, it is not safe to stay

And thus by alarming the brave and spirited, with the imputation of cowardice, the sober and prudent, with that of intemperance, and the liberal and magnificent, with parsimony and avarice, we incite them to laudable, and deter them from vicious pursuits. Where indeed there is no room for amendment we should shew ourselves remarkable for moderation and lenity, and our admonition should contain in it less of censure and rebuke, than of sorrow and commiseration but in stopping the career of vice and in combating with the passions, we ought to be urgent, implacable, and persevering. For this is the very season for exerting a firm and manly benevolence, and a real and genuine freedom. But in respect to censuring and reprimanding faults already committed, we see that even enemies pursue such a conduct towards each other thus Diogenes used to say, " that he who would be saved must have either " good friends, or violent enemies[68]," for the latter accuse, the former instruct But it is better for a man to guard against offence by listening to the admonition of his friends, than afterwards be forced to repentance, by the calumny and malice of his enemies And on this account we ought to use much art and circumspection in the application of reproof, inasmuch as it is the greatest and most powerful medicine in friendship, and not only requires a due and proper mixture, but dexterity in hitting the opportunity

Since therefore, as I have already observed, reproof is often grievous to the person reproved, let us imitate the conduct of the surgeons for neither do they after an operation leave the part affected in pain and anguish, but generally bathe and foment it in a mild and lenient manner, nor does the man, who knows how to admonish with propriety and affability, immediately desert his friend upon the application of rebuke and censure, but mitigates and softens his asperity by a milder and more lenient conversation like statuaries who smooth and polish off from their statues the rough and uncouth marks of the chissel and the hammer But if we forsake our friend, after we have wounded him with our censure, and leave him indignant and enraged at the treatment that he has received, we shall find it very difficult thereafter to restore him to ease and comfort And therefore a principal object to be attended to by those who admonish their friends is, not immediately to desert them upon it, nor to terminate their conversation and intercourse with the bitterness and severity of rebuke

F I N I S

REMARKS

ON

PLUTARCH'S TREATISE.

REMARKS

ON

PLUTARCH'S TREATISE, &c.

(1) W<small>HEN</small> we reflect that the passion of self-love is implanted in us by Nature, in all probability, for the best and wisest of purposes, the promotion of our happiness upon earth, we may surely without much difficulty admit the justice of Plato's observation, that a more than ordinary share of it is a venial fault. Self-love indeed seems to be a touchstone by which we try the wants of others, and it is from this source, as from a sacred fountain, that the rich streams of universal charity and benevolence take their rise. But this point of view has been set forth in such beauty and energy of language by that great poet and philosopher Mr. Pope, that I shall make no

hesitation in presenting the reader with a few of his inimitable lines.

> Self-love but serves the virtuous mind to wake,
> As the small pebble stirs the peaceful lake,
> The centre mov'd, a circle straight succeeds,
> Another still, and still another spreads;
> Friend, parent, neighbour, first it will embrace,
> His country next, and next all human race,
> Wide and more wide, th' o'erflowings of the mind
> Take every creature in of every kind,
> Earth smiles around, with boundless bounty blest,
> And Heav'n beholds its image in his breast.
> *Essay on Man Epist IV. ver.* 363

(2) At the same time however that we allow the passion of self-love, when kept under a proper subjection, to be of such eminent service to mankind, we should still be very careful so to moderate it by reason that it run not into excess, for beside the many evils to which in such a case we expose ourselves, it should be remembered that, " it is of " the ordonnance and constitution, as Dr War- " burton rightly observes, of all selfish passions, " when growing to excess, to defeat their own " end, which is self enjoyment." Here again the same immortal Poet, above cited, has shewn his thorough knowledge of man.

> Two principles in human nature reign,
> Self-love to urge, and Reason to restrain:
> Nor this a good, nor that a bad we call,
> Each works its end, to move or govern all.

And to their proper operation still,
Ascribe all good, to their improper ill
Warburton's Comment. on Pope's Mor Ess Epist II ver 1 *Essay on Man Epist II ver.* 53 *etc*

(3) We now come to one of the many ill consequences attendant upon the entertaining of too high an opinion of ourselves, which is, that it lays us open to the arts of evil-minded and designing men Our Moralist therefore very properly recommends us to imbibe a love of truth, by studying to *know ourselves*, for we shall discover such a mixture of frailties, follies, and vices blended with our virtues, and shall find, upon a review of our conduct, so many humiliating occasions of self-condemnation, as cannot fail of rendering us firm and inaccessible against the dangerous approaches of adulation* Plutarch in thus treating the subject of self-love has only trod in the footsteps of Cicero, who in his incomparable Essay upon Friendship, which the Attic translator Mr Melmoth has made his own, had observed that, " noxious as
" flattery is, no man was ever infected by it, who
" did not love and encourage the offering Accordingly there is no turn of mind so liable to
" be tainted by this sort of poison, as a disposition
" to entertain too high conceit of one's own me-
" rit I must confess at the same time, that con-

---

* I have used the words of the elegant Mr Melmoth, who in the above passage has translated or rather paraphrased a part of this treatise See p 55, and note on Melmoth's Lælius, p 133

" scious virtue cannot be void of self-esteem, as
" well knowing her own worth, and how amiable
" her form appears But the *pretenders* to virtue
" are much more numerous than the really vir-
" tuous, and it is of the former only that I am
" now speaking. Men of that character are par-
" ticularly delighted with adulation, as confirming
" their title, they imagine, to the merit they so
" vainly claim" *Melmoth's Lælius*, p 132.

(4) " I multiply, says Cicero, these equivalent
" terms, viz. flattery, compliment, and adulation,
" in order to mark with stronger emphasis the
" detestable and dangerous character of those pre-
" tended friends, who, strangers to the dictates of
" truth, constantly hold the language which they
" are sure will be most acceptable But if coun-
" terfeit appearances, of every species. are base
" and dishonest attempts to impose upon the
" judgement of the unwary, they are more pe-
" culiarly so in a commerce of amity, and abso-
" lutely repugnant to the vital principle of that
" sacred relation: for without sincerity, friend-
" ship is a mere name, that has neither meaning
" or efficacy." Now since truth and sincerity
are of such great importance in the intercourse of
friendship, that the connexion cannot exist without them, how cautious ought we ever to be in
the choice of friends, especially when we consider that the more open and unsuspicious our own

hearts are, the more easily do they fall a prey to the snares of the deceiver. On this account therefore, a strict attention to the rules of our Moralist cannot be too often nor too strenuously recommended, particularly to those in higher life, who from their elevated station become more exposed to the attacks of sycophants and parasites. Indeed I am convinced that there are few in such a situation who might not, *if they so willed*, be benefitted by the strong tests of flattery laid down in this treatise; but the misfortune is that the rich and powerful are too fond of adulation, and are apt to encourage " the easy companion, who either
" now and then throws out a little flattery, or lets
" a man silently flatter himself in his superiority
" to him. And if you take notice, there is hardly
" a rich man in the world, who has not such a led
" friend of small consideration, who is a darling for
" his insignificancy." When however I mention the caution to be observed in the choice of friends; I by no means wish to insinuate that there is any necessity for that haughtiness of carriage which savours more of pride and vanity than it does of a becoming regard to self-interest. No! I would have the golden mean studied in this, as in all other things,

Nolo nimis facilem, difficilemque nimis.

But we ought to remember that " it is the part of
' prudence to restrain a predilection from carry-
" ing us precipitately into the arms of a new friend,

" before we have, in some degree at least, put his
" moral qualifications to the test." *Melmoth's
Lælius, p. 95, and 127 Tatler, No. 208.*

(5) Adversity is most undoubtedly one of the great tests of friendship, and well might the Philosopher call that virtue almost more than human, that preserves its fidelity unshaken in the hour of distress.

> Scar'd at thy frown terrific, fly
> Self-pleasing Folly's idle brood,
> Wild Laughter, Noise, and thoughtless Joy,
> And leave us leisure to be good
> Light they disperse, and with them go
> The summer Friend *, the flattering Foe,
> By vain Prosperity receiv'd,
> To her they vow their truth, and are again believ'd
> *Gray's Ode to Adversity.*

And yet, though all history is clouded with examples, confirmed by daily experience, of the sad effects of a reverse of fortune upon the friends of the world, there are not wanting instances of the most approved constancy. Damon and Phintias were brought up in the Pythagorean philosophy, and entertained for each other so strict a friendship, that when Dionysius, the tyrant of Syracuse, had determined to put one of them to death, and the poor man begged only permission to go

---

* ———For men, like butterflies,
Shew not their mealy wings but to the summer
Shakspear, Troil. and Cress.

home and settle his affairs, the other hesitated not to give himself up as security for his return. The condemned person was accordingly liberated from prison, and his friend, to the admiration of Dionysius and his court, substituted in his room. Upon the approach of the day appointed, and the condemned not returning, every one began to blame the other for his rashness and folly. But he, not at all disheartened, strenuously affirmed that he doubted not of his friend's constancy, nor was he disappointed, for, at the very hour and moment fixt upon by Dionysius, his friend arrived. This so affected the tyrant that he not only granted a free pardon, but requested to be admitted into their friendship. *Val. Max. de Amicit. vinculo.*

(6) It is an observation not less general than true, that man is a social animal, and it is principally from this tendency of his nature that his chief happiness in life arises: for what is life itself or the pleasures of life, without a friend and companion to partake of the one, and alleviate the sorrows of the other? This idea is finely imagined by our divine Poet, who makes Adam, though in the apparently full possession of every earthly blessing, thus address his Maker

  O by what name, for thou above all these,
  Above mankind, or ought than mankind higher,
  Surpassest far my naming, how may I
  Adore thee, Author of this universe,
  And all this good to man? for whose well being

So amply, and with hands so liberal
Thou hast provided all things: but with me
I see not who partakes. In solitude
What happiness, who can enjoy alone,
Or all enjoying, what contentment find?
Thus I presumptuous——etc.
Paradise Lost, B viii ver. 357.

" I can only exhort you, says Cicero, to look on
" friendship as the most valuable of all human pos-
" sessions, no other being equally suited to the
" moral nature of man, or so applicable to every
" state and circumstance whether of prosperity or
" adversity, in which he can possibly be placed."
And again, " Life would be utterly *lifeless*, as old
" Ennius expresses it, without a friend on whose
" kindness and fidelity one might confidently re-
" pose." Indeed the necessity of friends to com-
plete our happiness upon earth is no where so ap-
parent as from the great multitude of flatterers;
for the very being of the latter may in some measure be accounted for from the great utility of the
former. But not to dwell upon a subject already
well known, I shall conclude this remark with a
quotation from Lord Bacon. " The parable of
" Pythagoras, observes that great Philosopher, is
" dark, but true, *Cor ne edito*, eat not the heart.
" Certainly, if a man would give it a hard phrase,
" those that want friends to open themselves unto,
" are cannibals of their own hearts. But one
" thing is most admirable, wherewith I will con-

'clude this first fruit of friendship, which is, that this communicating of a man's self to his friend works two contrary effects, for it redoubleth joys, and cutteth griefs in halfs. For there is no man that imparteth his joys to his friend, but he joyeth the more, and no man that imparteth his griefs to his friend, but he grieveth the less.' *Melmoth's Lælius*, p. 28, and 36 Lord Bacon's *Essay on Friendship*.

(7) That the tables of the rich have ever been constantly attended by sycophants and flatterers, is a truth that has seldom escaped the notice of the satirist* but Plutarch chiefly alludes in the present passage to that swarm of parasites *by trade*, with which Greece abounded, and which inundated into Rome after the fall of its liberty. 'Juvenal in one of his most animated satires, has directed the keenest poignancy of his wit and indignation against this supple and insidious tribe,' and that admirable poem has been imitated with such a congenial spirit in our own language, that I shall make no hesitation in presenting the reader with an extract from it.

* Who starves by Nobles, or with Nobles eats?
  The Wretch that trusts them, and the Rogue that cheats
  Is there a Lord, who knows a cheerful noon
  Without a Fiddler, Flatt'rer, or Buffoon?
  Whose table, Wit, or modest Merit share,
  Unelbow'd by a Gamester, Pimp, or Play'r.
     Pope's Mor. Essays, Epist.

The reader may compare above, remark the fourth

Studious to please, and ready to submit,
The supple *Gaul* was born a parasite
Still to his int'rest true, where-e'er he goes,
Wit, brav'ry, worth, his lavish tongue bestows.—

Practis'd their master's notions to embrace,
Repeat his maxims, and reflect his face,
With ev'ry wild absurdity comply,
And view each object with another's eye,
To shake with laughter ere the jest they hear,
To pour at will the counterfeited tear,
And as their patron hints the cold or heat,
To shake in dog-days, in December sweat.
Johnson's London.

The greater part of this remark is borrowed from Mr. Melmoth *, whose words, as being infinitely preferable to my own, I have made no scruple, with some slight variation, of adopting. I should however be very happy to transmute Dr Johnson's *Gaul,* into Juvenal's *Greek,* for, to say the truth, I abominate the keeping up of national antipathies, nor could I ever see what good end it answered. For the chief origin of the antipathy that exists between ourselves and our neighbours, we may look to the claim which we have long laid to the crown of France. " From this period (says Mr. Hume) " we may date the commencement of that great " animosity, which the English nation have ever " since borne to the French, which has so visible " an influence on all future transactions, and which

* See his Lælius, p. 317

" has been, and *continues to be*, the spring of many
" rash and precipitate resolutions among them."
See *Hume's Hist, vol* 11 *p* 397 *Octavo* 1778.

(8) It has ever been the great artifice and constant endeavour of the false friend, *to pry into our affairs, and get possession of our secrets*, well knowing that the poor unfortunate dupe to their hypocrisy has only one of these two evils to choose, *either be governed, or be betrayed* happy is it for him, if he has spirit enough to grasp the latter, and spurn the former.

> For arts like these preferr'd, admir'd, caress'd,
> They first invade your table, *then your breast*,
> Explore your secrets with insidious art,
> *Watch the weak hour*, and ransack all the heart,
> Then soon your ill-plac'd confidence repay,
> Commence your lords, and *govern or betray*.
> *Johnson's London.*

(9) Cicero in his oration pro Rege Deiotaro mentions a Latin verse * conveying the same meaning with this of the Greeks, and very justly calls it, *versus immanis, a savage sentiment*.

(10) The proverb here cited by Plutarch has also been applied by Cicero, who, speaking of friendship, observes that " not even fire and water are " capable of being converted to a greater variety " of beneficial purposes " and indeed, if we credit the same Philosopher when he asserts that, " if that

---

* Pereant amici dum una inimici intercidant.

" benevolent principle, which thus intimately unites
" two persons in the bands of amity, were to be
" struck out of the human heart, it would be im-
" possible that either private families, or public
" communities should subsist, even the land itself
" would lie waste, and desolation overspread the
" earth." I say that, if we credit this, there cannot
surely be a proposition that conveys a greater
truth. It is therefore with justice that Lord Bacon
remarks that, " without friends the world is but a
" wilderness."

> No Bandit fierce, no Tyrant mad with pride,
> No cavern'd Hermit, rests self-satisfied
> Who most to shun or hate mankind pretend,
> Seek an admirer, or would fix a friend
> Abstract what others feel, what others think,
> All pleasures sicken, and all glories sink
> Each has his share, and who would more obtain,
> Shall find the pleasure pays not half the pain

Melmoth's Lælius, p 37—8, 40. *Lord Bacon's Essay upon Friendship. Pope's Essay on Man* Epist iv ver 41.

(11) " Nothing in nature is so pliant and versa-
" tile as the genius of a flatterer, who always acts,
" and pretends to think in conformity, not only
" to the will and inclination, but even to the
" looks and countenance of another Like Gnatho
" in the play, he can prevail with himself to say
" either *yes* or *no,* as best suits the occasion, and

" he lays it down as his general maxim, never to
" dissent from the company." *Lælius, p. 128.*

(12) The Polypus is said to vary its whole figure at pleasure, and to catch its prey in the following manner. It lies in wait under some rock, the colour of which it assumes so exactly as to appear one and the same; when its destined prey approaches, it shoots out its tentacula or branches, and thus secures it. There is also a species of Hare, thence called variabilis, in the northern parts of Europe, which in winter changes its colour to a snowy whiteness, this change takes place in September, and the grey coat is resumed in April. The Chameleon is mentioned hereafter by our Author. *Ælian Var. Hist. de Polypode. Lib. I. Cap. 1. Encyc. Britan. Art. Lepus.*

(13) " To express at once, says Cicero, the whole
" spirit and essence of friendship, our inclina-
" tions, our sentiments, and our studies should be
" in perfect accord." And again, " Where our
' inclinations and pursuits are no longer similar,
" the true cement of friendship is dissolved. It
" is the total disparity between the disposition
" and manners of the virtuous and the vicious,
" that alone renders their coalition incompatible."
Lælius, p. 25, 108.

(14) Cicero lays it down as a fundamental axiom that, " true friendship can only subsist between

" those who are animated by the strictest prin-
" ciples of honour and virtue." And this great
truth the Philosopher most anxiously and repeat-
edly inculcates throughout the whole of his divine
essay upon friendship, nor does he seem to labour
in vain, for few after an attentive perusal of that
treatise will be so hardy as to deny that, " virtue is
" at once both the *parent* and *support* of friend-
" ship." Indeed there is something so amiable
and alluring in virtue that we cannot help being
" induced to desire a nearer and more intimate
" communion with the person in whom her lovely
" form appears, in order to enjoy those pure and
" mental advantages which flow from an habitual
" and familiar intercourse with the good." Nay
further, nature has implanted such a divine principle in our breasts that even where there can be no
hopes of intimacy or connexion, still are we cap-
tivated by the charms of virtue. Where is the man
whose heart doth not throb with philanthropy when
he hears of the beneficence of a Howard, who doth
not feel himself a patriot when he is informed of
the heroism of a Hambden?

It is true that there may exist confedera-
cies in vice, but no one surely in his senses
will dignify such with the exalted name of
friendship. it is interest alone which binds
them together, and the same interest will untie
them. " For they who persuade themselves that
" they may possess a true friend, at least, where
" moral merit has no share in producing the con-

" nexion, will find themselves miserably deceived,
" whenever some severe misfortune shall give
" them occasion to make the decisive experi-
" ment." *Lælius,* p 28, 34, 53, 119.

(15) The beard has ever been supposed a mark and emblem of wisdom, but to how little purpose the following epigram, quoted in the original by Mr. Krigel, and translated by my friend Mr. Wakefield, will clearly shew

> In length of beard and ragged coat
>   If so much sapience lies,
> E'en Plato's self yon aged goat
>   Would out-philosophize

(16) The variable, inconstant character attributed to Alcibiades is by no means uncommon in the world. Catiline was a notorious instance of that versatility of disposition that could accommodate itself to all persons, and all times Animus audax, subdolus, varius, cujuslibet rei simulator ac dissimulator, " A spirit that was daring, insidious, and shifting, expert in feigning what he meant not, and dissembling what he meant" *Gordon's Sallust*

But Mr. Pope has admirably well described this inconsistent character in the following lines,

> Wharton the scorn and wonder of our days,
> Whose ruling passion was the lust of praise

> Born with whate'er cou'd win it from the wise,
> Women and fools must like him or he dies,
> Tho' wond'ring senates hung on all he spoke,
> The club must hail him master of the joke
> Shall parts so various aim at nothing new?
> He'll shine a Tully and a Wilmot too
> Then turn repentant, and his God adores
> With the same spirit that he drinks and whores,
> Enough, if all around him but admire,
> And now the punk applaud, and now the fryer
>
> *Pope's Mor Essays, Ep 1 Ver. 180.*

(17) Dion the Syracusan Prince, and Brother-in-law of Dionysius, was a man of excellent abilities, and a professed admirer and follower of Plato, but through the intrigues of his enemies became so obnoxious to Dionysius, that the tyrant first ordered him to be imprisoned, and then banished him into Italy. Dion afterwards took up his residence in Athens, where he diligently attended the Academy, and profited much by the moral precepts of his master.

Enfield's Hist of Philosophy. B. 11. C viii

(18) Concerning the Polypus see note the twelfth, to which we may add that Aristotle confirms what is there remarked of that animal, respecting its assuming the colour of the rock to which it approaches, and that it does this not only for the purpose of obtaining food, but for that of avoiding its enemies. It has also the same power as

the Cuttle-fish, of issuing a black turbid liquor. The following lines of Ovid well describe the Polypus.

> At contra scopulis crinali corpore segnis
> Polypus hæret, et hac eludit retia fraude,
> Et sub lege loci sumit mutatque colorem,
> Semper ei similis quem contigit.
>
> *Aristot. Hist Animal Lib. IX Cap.* 37
> *Ovid. Halieut.* 30.

(19) Nothing surely is so despicable in itself, and degrading to man, as that pliant and supple character which dares not openly avow its sentiments, but depends entirely upon the will of another. Human nature in a person of this stamp is reduced to a level with that of the brute creation, inasmuch as he lays aside the great prerogative and characteristic of man, Reason. " Terence
" exposes this baseness of soul, in the person of
" a contemptible parasite, but how much more
" contemptible (says Cicero) does it appear, when
" exhibited in the conduct of one who dares
" usurp the name of friend." Now as I have already enlarged upon this subject, (see above, notes 4 and 7) I have only to add that the best means of detecting this baseness is, to keep in mind that, " One of the principal ingredients to
" form the character of a true friend, is a steadi-
" ness and constancy of temper."

Lælius, p. 128, 94.

(20) Cicero, who has made a masterly inquiry into the question, how far the claims of friendship may reasonably extend? has laid it down as a rule without exception, " that no degree of friendship " can either justify, or excuse, the commission of " a criminal action For true amity being founded " on an opinion of virtue in the object of our " affection, it is scarcely possible that those senti- " ments should remain, after an avowed and open " violation of the principles which originally " produced them.—Let it be established therefore, " continues the Philosopher, as one of the most " sacred and indispensible laws of this connexion, " never either to make, or to grant a request which " honour and virtue will not justify " And here I cannot but hope that the reader will pardon the frequency of my quotations upon this subject, but its great truth and importance are so deeply impressed upon my mind, that I am convinced it is owing to a want of attention to this principle, that we are so often hearing complaints of the violation of amity. It is moreover from the same source that the sacred name of friend has come to signify only an acquaintance. Let us therefore in every intercourse of this sort carefully retain in our memory that, virtue is the chief object which we ever should have in view, and that friendship is only second to it. *Lælius, p.* 61, 64

(21) But the flatterer does not rest satisfied with only copying our vices, his great care is, that we have no virtues, for, well knowing that virtue and wisdom are so nearly allied that they are almost convertible terms, one of his chief artifices in order to entice our affections to himself, and from our real friends is, that of endeavouring to draw us aside from the paths of science and philosophy, for such forsooth! are unworthy of the pursuit of a *gentleman*, whose *sole* business and occupation should be one continued routine of pleasure and amusement. Thus secondaries often become primaries, and the ignorance of men, as some one says, is made their pride. But to prevent this infection from spreading, I will beg leave to remind my reader of what has been aptly quoted by a modern writer from the book of Proverbs *Wisdom is the principal thing, therefore get wisdom, and with all thy getting get understanding.*

(22) Nothing surely in nature can be so unreasonable, and contrary to the genuine spirit of true friendship, as that captious disposition which is ever finding fault with the trivial offences of others, and yet, it must with sorrow be confessed that, we are all more or less infected with it, for the truth is that mankind in general are so apt to think highly of themselves, that they claim, as it were, a title to reprove others. But perhaps it would not be amiss, if some of us, at least, were to bear in mind the divine maxim of our Saviour, "Thou hypocrite,

"first cast out the *beam* out of thine own eye; and
"then shalt thou see clearly to cast out the *mote*
"out of thy brother's eye." There is a fine passage of Plutarch to this purpose, which I shall give to the reader in the words of the Attic Melmoth, as it is cited by him in his remarks on Lælius "If
"the man who is inclined to animadvert with too
"much severity on the failings of others, would
"turn his eyes inward, and honestly ask his heart,
"*was I never guilty of the same?* the true answer
"to that question, could not fail to render him
"less observant of those little pardonable defects
"in the characters of his connexions, at which he
"is apt to take such quick offence." *Lælius, p.* 312.

(23) Here certainly is a very strong reason why
"we should not suffer *affection* to take root in our
"hearts before *judgment* has time to interpose."
"For the first fruit of friendship being, as Lord
"Bacon says, "the ease and discharge of the ful-
"ness and swellings of the heart," if we do not well examine into the moral merit of the person whom we are to admit into our affections, we shall very soon have occasion to lament our *ill-placed confidence* *. It is more perhaps from this single article of breach of trust, that the frequent dissolutions of friendship arise, than from any other source whatever And what can possibly shew the moral depravity of another in a stronger light, than ex

---

* Compare remark the eighth.

posing the secrets of one who trusted him? But the great misfortune is, that the generality of men are so much given to calumny and misrepresentation, and imagine that their own cause is so much promoted by the ruin of their neighbour's, and at the same time perhaps their reason is so clouded by their passion, that they forget, in their resentment, the horrid impiety of exposing what may have been revealed to them under the sacred roof of friendship

> ———Absentem qui rodit amicum,
> Qui non defendit, alio culpante, solutos
> Qui captat risus hominum, famamque dicacis,
> Fingere qui non visa potest, commissa tacere
> Qui nequit, hic niger est, hunc tu, Romane, caveto
> *Hor. Sat* iv *Lib.* 1 *ver* 81.

For the following elegant translation of the above passage of Horace, I am indebted to my learned friend Mr. Wakefield.

> Who smites with sland'rous tongue his absent friend,
> Or shuns his injur'd honour to defend,
> Who builds on low buffoonery his fame,
> And emulates a babbling coxcomb's name,
> Who *blabs the secret, coins the blasting lye,*
> That wretch let ev'ry gen'rous Briton fly.
> *Lælius, p* 119 *Bacon's Essay upon Friendship.*

(24) "A flatterer of this insidious and concealed
" kind, says Cicero, will frequently gain his point
" even by opposition he will affect to maintain
" opinions which he does not hold, and dispute

"in order to give you the credit of a victory." But there is another species of flattery, the ingenuity of which is still more refined. A man of this sort, for instance, in his praises or censures of good or bad actions, will often add some such clause as the following, *as you, my friend, were observing the other day* thus giving you the credit of an observation, which you not only never made, but perhaps, if capable of making, never had in idea. By such insinuating means the reptile attempts to wind himself into our good graces, and to the disparagement of real amity is too frequently successful. In truth, to repeat what has been before remarked, we are all of us so fond of commendation, that we choose not to give ourselves the trouble of inquiring, *whether we deserve it.* *Lalius,* p. 135.

(25) "When the braggart Captain in the play
" asks Gnatho, Did Thais return me many thanks,
" say you? An artless man would have thought
" it sufficient to answer *many*, but the cunning
" sycophant replies, *immense, innumerable* for a
" skilful flatterer perfectly well knows, that a pleas-
" ing circumstance can never be too much exag-
" gerated, in the opinion of the person upon
" whom he means to practise." *Lælius,* p. 134-5.

(26) Cicero, to shew his contempt of that serious, tragedy-like, deportment which is always disposed to censure even the temperate relaxation of others, has not scrupled to put the following sentiments

into the mouth of the rigid, severe, inflexible Cato. "I would not however be thought so pro-
" fessed an enemy to the latter, (the pleasures of
" the palate) as to deny that, within certain limits,
" they may very reasonably, perhaps, be indulged:
" and I declare, for the satisfaction of those who
" are unwilling to part with this kind of gratifica-
" tions, that I do not find old age is a disqualifi-
" cation for the enjoyment of them." *Melmoth's Cato, p.* 70. See the excellent remark of Melmoth on the above passage.

(27) There cannot exist a better mode of detecting the flatterer, than by casting our eyes to the *end* that he has in view, and the *means* which he uses to obtain that end: and we shall ever find the first to be his own interest, however remote and concealed; and the second, whatever he thinks will be grateful and acceptable to the object of his pursuit. How different is such a conduct from that of the real friend: his sole aim is our advantage, and that frequently at the expence of much comfort to himself, and the means that he employs to obtain his purpose, though perhaps harsh and grating, yet, like the chidings of a fond mother, charm in the midst of frowns.

" The counsels of a faithful and friendly moni-
" tor, says Cicero, carry with them an authority
" which ought to have great influence, and they
" should be urged not only with freedom but even

"with severity, if the occasion should appear to
"require it." For thus the Bee sometimes indeed
stings, but oftener produces honey. *Lælius*, p. 70—1.

(28) Plutarch, in the course of this treatise, both frequently and strongly inculcates the necessity of lenient measures in a commerce of friendship, and in this he only follows the footsteps of most of the ancient Philosophers. Cicero has carried this subject further; and has observed that, even in circumstances which render it expedient for a man of honour to break with his friend, (either from some latent vice or concealed ill-humour unexpectedly discovering itself) the most adviseable and prudent conduct is, to suffer the intimacy to wear out by silent and insensible degrees; or, to use a strong expression of Cato, "the bands of
"friendship should be gradually untied rather than
"suddenly cut asunder." *See Lælius, p.* 110—1.

(29) Thus Aristippus told certain of his friends, who were upon some occasion overwhelmed with grief, that he came not to join their lamentations, but to put an end to them. *Ælian Var Hist. Lib* vii. *cap* 3

(30) "There is one particular duty, says Cicero,
"which may frequently occur, and which a true
"friend will at all hazards of offence discharge;
"as it is never to be superseded consistently with
"the truth and fidelity he owes to the connexion,

" I mean the duty of admonishing and even re-
" proving his friend an office which, whenever it
" is affectionately exercised, should be kindly re-
" ceived It must be confessed however that the
" remark of my dramatic friend is too frequently
" verified, who observes in his Andria, that *obse-*
" *quiousness conciliates friends, but truth creates*
" *enemies*" The real fact is, that we are so accustomed, as has been often observed, to entertain
a good opinion of ourselves, that we attribute all
our misfortunes rather to fate and chance, than
suffer ourselves to be persuaded to consider
them as the effect of our own rashness and impru-
dence *Lælius, p* 124.

(31) This passage in the original is so extremely
obscure that it has puzzled all the commentators
and critics. I have therefore chosen rather to give
the reader the general meaning, than attempt a verbal translation My friend Mr Wakefield has indeed with his usual acuteness explained the passage
much to my satisfaction, but as I have purposely
avoided all Greek criticism in this work, I shall
not here break my original design, but shall reserve
what I have to say upon this and many other pas-
sages, until I publish the original, which, being
a favourite treatise, I have some intention of doing
Indeed I look upon Greek criticism in a translation of a moral treatise, as a breach of good manners Græcum est, non potest legi

The Ptolemy here mentioned most probably is Auletes, so called from his playing upon the flute, and so thinks Gesner. Others suppose that Philopater is intended, but I am induced to believe the former, not only because the flute is afterwards mentioned as belonging to him, but on account of the general character of the man for effeminacy and superstition. *See Universal Hist. under Ptolemy Auletes*

(32) The dignified appellations with which the virtues (however trivial) of great men are saluted, bring to my mind the following lines of Pope.

'Tis from high life high characters are drawn
A Saint in crape is twice a Saint in lawn;
A Judge is just, a Chanc'llor juster still,
A Gownsman, learn'd, a Bishop, what you will
Wife, if a Minister, but, if a King,
More wise, more learn'd, more just, more ev'ry thing

(33) This line is taken from the Comedy of Menander, entitled the Flatterer; and the spirit of the passage seems to consist in this, that the parasite Struthias attributes to the praise of Bias, what was the disgrace of Alexander. The fragment as quoted by Le Clerc from Athenæus may be thus translated.

BIAS.   In Cappadocia thrice did I quaff off
    A golden goblet, Struthias, that contain'd
    Near twice five pints.

S TRUTH Not Alexander's self
Could drink so much. B. 'Tis true by Jupiter.
S T RUTH 'Twas great indeed.

I have followed Dr. Bentley's emendations, and have only added Bias as the other speaker, which had escaped the notice of that bright luminary of Britain.

(34) Plutarch, from a deficiency of good manuscripts, abounds in difficulties and obscurities, and the passage before us is so strong an instance of it, that the celebrated Mr. Reiske says, it is better at once to confess the obscurity, than attempt any useless conjecture. I shall only add that the learned commentator upon this treatise, Mr. Krigel, supposes, that by the Cyprian is meant the luxurious and prodigal Nicocles King of Cyprus.

(35) In all ages of luxury, the morals of the people are so depraved, that they are wont to pay that adoration to external wealth and pomp, which is due only to internal worth and virtue. nor do I think, with respect to my own country, that *all the preaching in the world* will prevent the evil from spreading, unless the Legislature take upon itself the important task of forming a plan of public education. As it is not however my present purpose to expatiate upon this fruitful topic, the above hint must suffice.

O Cives, Cives, quærenda pecunia primum
Virtus post nummos.

Wealth's the chief object that we all adore
And virtue only ranks in second place.

(36) Ælian, who relates this story in his Various History, makes the painter's name Zeuxis. But to shew the folly of pretending to judge of what we do not understand, I shall present the reader with another story of the same sort, and told by the same author. Alexander being once at Ephesus, and seeing his own portrait drawn by Apelles, did not admire it according to its merit, but upon a horse being brought up to it, and neighing at his own image (which the painter had introduced upon the canvas) as if it had been a real animal, "Certainly, O King, said Apelles, this "horse appears to have much more skill than "you in the art of painting." *Ælian Var Hist Lib.* II. *Cap.* 3.

(37) It would appear invidious to expatiate upon this too-fertile subject. I shall therefore only present the reader with an extract from Mr Melmoth's first remark upon Lælius. That elegant and accomplish'd writer is treating of the degeneracy of the Roman manners after the destruction of the ancient republic, and the author*, from

---

* Auctor dialog. de caus. corrupt. eloquent.

whom his representation is taken, complains, "that
"all conversation was so universally infected with
"topics of this unworthy nature, (horse-races,
"gladiatorial shews, etc.) that they were the con-
"stant subjects of discourse, not only amongst
"the youth in their seminaries, but even of their
"tutors themselves. For it was not, he remarks,
"by stricter morals, or superior genius, that this
"order of men gained disciples, it was by the
"meanest compliances with their pupils, and the
"most servile adulation of their patrons." I very
earnestly recommend the whole remark, which is
upon the education of the Romans, to the perusal
of the reader.

(38) "Another rule likewise, says Cicero, of
"indispensible obligation, upon all who would
"approve themselves true friends, is, to be ever
"ready to offer their advice with an unreserved
"and honest frankness of heart." *Lælius*, p 70.

(39) Not much unlike this sort of flatterers, is
that mentioned by Horace

Sæpe tribus lectis videas cœnare quaternos
E quibus unus avet quâvis aspergere cunctos,
Præter eum qui præbet aquam post, hunc quoque potus,
Condita cum verax aperit præcordia Liber
Hic tibi comis, et urbanus, liberque videtur
Infesto nigris. *Sat. Lib.* 1. 4. 86.

At tables, crowded with a dozen guests,
Some one shall scatter round his frigid jests,
And only spare his host, until the bowl,
Fair friend of truth, unlocks his inmost soul
Yet tho' a cruel joker you detest,
He seems a courteous, well-bred, easy guest.
Francis

(40) In my translation of this passage I have followed the Latin version of Erasmus, but with all due deference to so great a character, I do not think that the words of the original will bear such an interpretation. Reiske suspects some error in the manuscript. As however I have already hinted that it is not my present purpose to launch out into verbal criticism, I shall postpone what little I have to say upon the original to some future opportunity.

(41) This remark of our Moralist is not only true, when the flatterer *sees* brothers and friends at variance, but often when he *sees them not* at variance: for in order to *create* dissention, and separate a man from his real and true friend, (which by the bye is always the *first* concern of the flatterer) he will tell him, *to think more highly of his own importance, and not be so obsequious and submissive, that it is time now to throw away his leading strings, and to judge for himself*, and such like. By this artifice he sometimes, too frequently indeed, obtains his desired purpose, gets him under

his own power, and *becomes himself his conductor*. The best mode of escaping from this snare is, in the words of Plutarch*, *to consider the end in view*, that is, whether the advice of the flatterer be given for his own, or for your advantage. For, as Lord Shaftesbury observes upon another occasion, " it is no easy matter to make advice a free gift, for to make a gift free indeed, there must be nothing in it *which takes from another, to add to ourself* †." *Advice to an Author*.

(42) That wine will destroy the poisonous quality of hemlock has been asserted by Pliny, Macrobius, and others, and to this purpose a story is told by Plutarch, in his Essay upon Loquacity, of some robbers who had plundered a temple of Minerva in Lacedæmon, and had each of them previous to the attempt, drunk a draught of hemlock, and taken the precaution to bring a flaggon of wine with them, to the intent that, if they escaped, they might destroy the force of the poison by drinking the wine, and that, if they were apprehended, they might die by means of the poison, and thus avoid torture.

---

* Compare above, Remark 27.

† " It is a rare thing, saith Lord Bacon, except it be from a perfect and entire friend, to have counsel given, but such as shall be bowed and crooked to some ends which he hath that giveth it." *Essay on Friendship*.

(43) "It is virtue, (says Cicero) yes, let me re-
"peat it again, it is virtue alone that can give birth,
"strength, and permanency to friendship." Indeed
this subject is such a favourite with that great Philosopher that he seldom or never loses sight of it throughout the whole of his divine essay upon friendship. But not to overload the reader with quotations, I will beg leave to refer him to remark the 14th and 20th   *Lælius,* p. 137

(44) The meaning of this passage will be best explained by a note of Mr Brewster's upon the following lines of his elegant translation of Persius.

> Behold then, undismay'd by threaten'd ill,
> Spite of all saving counsel, bathe he will
> Tho' his pale belly, pamp'ring dainties bloat
> And noisome fumes rise ling'ring from his throat.

"The general custom was, to bathe before meals,
"but riotous gluttons bathed also after meals, in
'order to procure sudden digestion, instead of
"which, they were sometimes visited with sudden
"death"   *Persius,* Sat III v 240.

(45) Cicero remarks that, "in a commerce of
"friendship, mutual requests or concessions should
"neither be made nor granted, without due and
"mature deliberation." And indeed nothing can be more just than this maxim, or more conformable to that sacred law of amity which commands

us, " never to require from a friend what he can-
" not grant without a breach of his honour, and al-
" ways to be ready to assist him upon every oc-
" casion consistent with that principle." Here
then we have an admirable touchstone of the flatterer, who always attaches to the irrational and
depraved part of man, (see above, p 41—2) and
whose whole strength and energy consist in our
weakness. How sensible then ought we to be of
the value of a real and true friend, who will strenuously exert himself in keeping our eyes open
to the dictates of reason and virtue, and consequently guard us against the bewitching snares of
the deceiver *Lælius,* p 70, 110.

(46) According to Diogenes Laertius who relates this story, (*Lib* IV *Segm* 37) it was not
Apelles the Chian, but Ctesibius, a native of Chalcis,
who was benefited by the liberality of Arcesilaus,
nor is the particular sum mentioned, but merely a
purse.

(47) It is one of the greatest advantages of true
philosophy, that it infuses a love of virtue into the
breasts of its followers. Plato, through the intrigues of Dionysius, had been sold as a slave upon
the island of Ægina, and in this state was discovered by Anicerris, a Cyrenaic philosopher, " who,
" thinking himself happy in an opportunity of shew-
" ing his respect for so illustrious a person, pur-
" chased his freedom for thirty minæ, and sent him

" home to Athens. Repayment being afterwards
" offered to Anicerris by Plato's relations, he re-
" fused the money, saying, with that generous spirit
" which true philosophy always inspires, that he saw
" no reason why the relations of Plato should en-
" gross to themselves the honour of serving him."
True! for that genuine glow of the Divinity which
every good man feels in the conscious satisfaction
of having done an act of benevolence, more than
amply compensates any inconvenience that may
have attended the performance of it. See *Enfield's
Hist of Philosophy. B* ii *Ch* viii *S* 1.

(48) The manner in which this story is related
by Plutarch evidently shews that it met his approbation, but how far the reader will agree with the
Philosopher it is not for me to determine, nor shall
I attempt to solve the question, how far Justice may
yield to Friendship thus much indeed may be risked
with safety, that if any thing in this world be ex-
cusable, it is Enthusiasm in this *best affection of
the human heart*. Even Cicero (see above, note
20,) ventures to assert that, " in cases where the
" life, or good fame, of a friend is concerned, it
" may be allowable to deviate a little from the
" path of strict right in order to comply with his
" desires, provided, however, that by this com
" pliance our own character be not materially
" affected." The reader who is desirous of seeing
a more accurate investigation of this subject may

compare the remark of the elegant and accomplished Mr. Melmoth upon the above passage, with the same writer's 28th letter of Fitzosborne *Lælius*, *p* 93.

(49) " To be capable, says Cicero, of reproaching a man with the obligations you have conferred upon him is a disposition exceedingly contemptible and odious it is *his* part indeed not to forget the good offices he has received, but ill, certainly, would it become his friend to be the monitor for that purpose." Mr. Gibbon too, in his admirable History of the Decline and Fall of the Roman Empire, very justly observes that, " the most lively resentment is excited by the tyranny of pretended benefactors, who sternly exact the debt of gratitude which they have cancelled by subsequent injuries." Still something may be advanced upon the other side of the question that deserves to be attended to. Mankind are but too prone to forget benefits conferred, and though ever ready to receive favours, yet that friend is often a troublesome companion who requires any return. Virgil therefore, who well knew human nature, puts these words into the mouth of Ilioneus, when addressing king Latinus,

———Nec tanti abolescet gratia facti
Æn vii. 232

Nor Latium shall repent the kind supply,
Nor shall the dear remembrance ever die.
Pitt.

Lælius, p. 105   *Gibbon, vol* iv *p* 386

(50) It is on this account that Cicero recommends a man's first endeavour to be, " to acquire " himself those moral excellencies which consti- " tute a virtuous character, and then to find an as- " sociate whose good qualities reflect back the " true image of his own." *Lælius, p.* 116. Compare above, note 14.

(51) This metaphor is very frequently used by the ancient Poets and Philosophers, and as it is applied with the happiest effect in the following lines of Persius I shall make no scruple of laying them before the reader.

> ———Sonat vitium percussa, maligne
> Respondet, viridi non cocta fidelia limo.
> Udum et molle lutum es, nunc, nunc properandus, et acri
> Fingendus sine fine rota.———*Sat.* iii 21

> The ill-bak'd jar, if rung, will sound its fault
> The finger's test proclaims the vessel naught
> Such wilt thou be, as yet obedient clay,
> Soft and impressive   Form, without delay,
> Form it, submit it to the potter's wheel
> *Now,* let it *now* the plastic finger feel   *Brewster*

(52) I do not imagine that Plutarch here means that perfect friend, whom Aristotle and others have defined, a *second-self,* or, as Lord Bacon says, *far more than himself,* for such friendship " is ex- " erted for the benefit of only two or three per- " sons at the utmost," but the Moralist in all probability means such a friend whom a man may love

and revere, and from whom he may expect a like return Indeed the first species of friendship, which was carried almost to enthusiasm by the Ancients, is seldom to be met with among the Moderns, and this chiefly arises from the difference of education, " for while the greatest geniuses among them em- " ployed their talents in exalting this noble affec- " tion, and it was encouraged even by the laws " themselves, what effects might one not expect to " arise from the concurrence of such powerful " causes?" I would not however be understood to infer that there does not exist among the Moderns a very exalted and amiable species of friendship, but only that we seldom or never meet with that refined connexion which existed between Nisus and Euryalus, Pylades and Orestes. Achilles and Patroclus, Lælius and Scipio, to which we may add Cicero and Atticus, and several others *Lælius, p* 33 *Fitzosborne, Lett* 28

(53) Calumny and misrepresentation are so much in vogue at the present moment, that one would imagine the soul of Medius to have transmigrated, and himself to be now prescribing in full practice Joking apart, it is but too true that the scar of slander will long remain after the wound is healed. But surely it would be no difficult matter to stop the progress of these murderers of reputation, if we would but resolutely determine to hear no tale that derogates from the good fame of another, without

at the same time inquiring what that other may have to say in his own defence. The rule is simple, may be easily retained, and, if attended to, would obviate a great deal of mischief. Indeed the man who is unwilling to suspend his judgment till he has heard both sides of the question, is himself next of kin to the calumniator. This truth cannot be too forcibly impressed upon our minds, because it imports us to recollect that it is the nature of envy to attack only the laudable character* That virtue which is seated above its reach, it will endeavour to bring down to its level, which it cannot emulate, it will strive to depress. Nor is this all, the tooth of calumny does not bite once or twice, but gnaws to eternity, it is like the fall of a cataract, by perpetual impulse it wears through a rock of adamant

(54) Hence it is that the Apostate Julian used to say that he exulted in the commendation of those men who dared also reprove him when he did amiss. And indeed so true is it that our follies and vices stand in need of the corrective hand of friendship, that it almost appears as if we were indebted to them for the origin of friendship itself

* Ἀπλέται δ' ἐσθλῶν ἀεί,
  Χειρόνεσσι δ' ἐκ ἐρίζει.   *Pind. Nem.* 8.

Since living virtue is with envy curs'd,
And the best men are treated like the worst
                        Pope. Tem of Fame, 320

> Wants, frailties, passions, closer still ally
> The common interest, or endear the tie,
> To these we owe true friendship, love sincere,
> Each home-felt joy that life inherits here
>
> *Pope Ess on Man, Ep ii ver 253*

Lord Bacon has well observed that, "the best preservative to keep the mind in health, is the faithful admonition of a friend The calling of a man's self to a strict account, is a medicine sometimes too piercing and corrosive Reading good books of morality, is a little flat and dead Observing our faults in others, is sometimes improper for our case but the best receipt, best, I say, to work, and best to take, is the admonition of a friend" But how serviceable soever this receipt may be to those who are able and willing to take it, yet I am afraid that, upon an impartial investigation of the subject, it will be found, to many of us at least, a nauseous and bitter draught for the misfortune is that, "we hate the admonition and love the vice, whereas we ought, on the contrary, to hate the vice and love the admonition" *Ammian Lib xxii cap 10 Bacon's Essay on Friendship Lælius, p.* 126.

(55) "Nothing is more suitable, says Cicero, to the genius and spirit of true friendship, than to give and receive advice, to give it, I mean, with freedom, but without rudeness, and to receive it, not only without reluctance, but with patience" *Lælius, p* 126

(56) The aurea mediocritas, the medio tutissimus, the golden mean, are in the mouth of every body, but though we be ever ready to allow the truth of the observation, that virtue lies equally distant from the opposite vices, yet how few of us are there that follow it up by practice.

The reader may compare the above passage of Plutarch with the beginning of the 18th Epistle of the first book of Horace.

(57) This certainly is a very valuable maxim, and evidently points out our real duty, happy is it when we have strength enough to practise it, but motives of interest and the gratification of revenge are powerful opponents to duty, these are wont to supply us with the seeds of calumny, which the generality of us are but too apt to scatter with a liberal hand. But such is the weakness of human nature, let it rather excite our compassion than our anger.

(58) This reproof was manifestly too severe to be borne by such a tyrant as Dionysius and this the reader will clearly perceive by a little insight into the history. Harmodius and Aristogiton were both citizens of Athens, and united in the strictest bands of amity. Enraged on account of a public affront put upon them by Hipparchus, one of the tyrants of Athens, they formed the desperate resolution of liberating their country from the tyranny both of him and his brother Hippias. The

festival of the Panathenæa was the time fixt upon for the enterprize, but they were so far frustrated in their design, that though they destroyed Hipparchus, yet his brother Hippias found means to quell the conspiracy, and both the friends were put to death. Afterwards, upon the restoration of the liberties of Athens, extraordinary honours were paid to their memory, their names were held in almost equal reverence with those of the gods, and statues were erected to them in the market place. *Rollin, vol* ii *p* 325, 327.

(59) Thus it is read in the fragments of Pindar, and thus were those gods called who were said to avert evil, and what appellation could better become the jolly God of wine? Moreover, Suidas informs us that Lysian feasts were those of Bacchus, and that the Bœotians built a temple to Lysian Bacchus. Hesychius too expressly says, that Bacchus was called Lysian. I hope the learned reader will have the goodness to pardon this critical remark, as I deemed it absolutely necessary to vindicate the present reading against that of most other editions, which have it Lydian.

(60) " Weak minds, says Cicero, elated with be-
" ing distinguished by the smiles of fortune, are
" generally disposed to assume an arrogant and
" supercilious demeanour*, and there is not in

---

* Stultitiam patiuntur opes   *Hor*
  In Nobles folly has a sort of grace   *Neville*

"the whole compass of nature a more insufferable
"creature than a prosperous fool." Indeed it is so
common an observation that mankind are apt to be
elated by prosperity, that there are few moral writers whose notice it has escaped. Plutarch therefore well observes that the rich stand in the greatest
need of friends to depress that elevation of mind.
But the great evil is, that what a man stands most
in need of, he is often the least likely to obtain,
for " he may be flattered indeed by his followers
" with the specious semblance of personal attach-
" ment; but whenever he falls, it will appear
" how totally destitute he stood of every genuine
" friend." *Lælius*, p 83—4.

(61) That is, because such a demeanour had a
tendency to banish all his friends from him. Thus
Cicero very much doubts whether the imperious
Tarquin, (who used to say in his exile that " his
" misfortunes had taught him to discern his real
" from his pretended friends,") ever had a sincere
friend; for, independent of all haughtiness of carriage, " it frequently happens that the being ad-
" vanced into exalted stations, proves the occa-
" sion of excluding the great and powerful from
" possessing that inestimable felicity." But as the
great Historian Mr. Gibbon remarks of the active
mind of Belisarius, that " in the pride of victory it
" could suppose a defeat," so let us too *in the pride
of wealth suppose poverty*. See *Lælius*, p 83.

(62) Undoubtedly the most effectual mode of silencing the tongue of calumny is, *to live as in the presence of an enemy* but such strict circumspection is, I fear, scarcely compatible with the frailty of human nature. Man being composed of two parts, there are and must be times when the weaker will get the better of the stronger, when our passions will overstep the bounds prescribed by our reason. These are the opportunities which the vigilance of the enemy instantly seizes hold of, and as he always looks through a microscopic medium, every mole-hill is magnified into a mountain, and there is no failing, be it ever so trifling, than can escape his penetration.

(63) The Greeks in general were exceedingly temperate in their manner of living. the Lacedæmonians indeed, while they observed the laws of Lycurgus, were so noted for their temperance, that the black broth peculiar to that nation, became a sort of stigma upon them. But upon this head I beg leave to refer my reader to Archbishop Potter's Antiquities of Greece *Book* iv *Chap* 18

(64) It certainly savours more of arrogance, and littleness of mind, than of the genuine spirit of real amity, to reprove the faults of our friend before witnesses, nor indeed has such admonition the desired effect, for instead of reforming the morals, it serves only in general to exasperate and inflame the passions. Possibly however it may be

objected to this reasoning, that circumstances may occur which render it absolutely necessary for a man to admonish his friend in the presence of others. Granted, but surely we may do this without exposing him; there are a thousand ways of mitigating the asperity of reproof, which nature herself points out, by the eye, by the gesture, by the tone of voice, that will be found infinitely more effectual in their operation than all the censures in the world.

(65) This story is told more at length by Valerius Maximus. Polemo, a young Athenian of the most dissolute and abandoned morals, returning home once from a feast, which he had left not after the setting, but after the rising of the sun, observed the door of Xenocrates open, and staggering through inebriety, smeared with ointment, his head crowned with garlands, and apparelled in a white robe *, entered in this plight the school of the Philosopher, who was at that time giving lectures to an audience of literary men. Not content with the indecency of this intrusion, he began to mock and ridicule the sublime discourse and wise precepts that were delivered. The indignation of the whole company was roused to the highest pitch, but Xenocrates kept his counte-

* For the various ceremonies at the entertainments of the Ancients see *Potter's Antiq. Book* iv *ch.* 20.

nance unmoved, and changed the subject of his discourse to that of temperance and modesty. The weight of this had such an effect upon Polemo, that he first tore off the crown from his head, soon after, withdrew his arm within his robe *, lay aside the gaiety of his countenance, and at last stripping off every emblem of luxury, by the wholesome medicine of one single discourse, from the most infamous debauchee turned out the greatest philosopher. His mind sojourned in vice, but fixt not its habitation there. *Valer. Max. Lib.* vi. *cap.* 9.

(66) If a man be thoroughly convinced of the good intentions of his friend, it is certainly his duty to listen to him with patience, and bear quietly with his admonition, for if he feel sore and impatient under the correction, it serves only to shew his guilt or folly in a stronger light. Rien n'est beau que le vrai, " desperate then indeed
" must that man's moral disorders be, who shuts
" his ears to the voice of truth, when delivered by
" a sincere and affectionate monitor." *Lælius,*
p. 125.

(67) Cicero,

Whose own example strengthens all his laws,

has fully confirmed the truth of this remark in his

---

* This was a mark of shame and modesty among the Athenians

incomparable Essay upon Old Age. " Age, says
" that Philosopher, brings along with it experi-
" ence, discretion and judgement*," and what
greater good can there be bestowed upon man
than that which derives from these three? The respect which the Spartans paid to years may be
learnt from the story so well related in the sixth
number of the Spectator, to which I beg leave to
refer the reader, and surely it must be owing to
a depraved education that grey hairs are so little
reverenced in modern times. *Melmoth's Cato;*
p 103.

(68) Plutarch has written an excellent treatise
upon the advantages to be derived from our enemies, and as every good and upright man must ne-
cessarily excite the hatred and malice of the evil-

---

*———————Non omnis grandior ætas,
Quæ fugiamus, habet seris venit usus ab annis
Ovid Met vi 28.

Αἰεὶ δ᾽ ὁπλοτέρων ἀνδρῶν φρένες ἠερέθονται·
Οἷς δ᾽ ὁ γέρων μετέῃσιν, ἅμα πρόσσω καὶ ὀπίσσω
Λεύσσει, ὅπως ὄχ᾽ ἄριστα μετ᾽ ἀμφοτέροισι γένηται
Iliad γ 108

Let reverend Priam in the truce engage,
And add the sanction of considerate age,
His sons are faithless, headlong in debate,
And youth itself an empty wav'ring state.
Cool age advances venerably wise,
Turns on all hands its deep-discerning eyes,
Sees what befel, and what may yet befal,
Concludes from both, and best provides for all
Pope.

minded, and consequently create to himself a number of enemies, the good reader will thank me for recommending it to his serious perusal. In this tract the speech here attributed to Diogenes, is given to Antisthenes. And Cicero has remarked that, " it was a saying of Cato, that some men
" were more obliged to their inveterate enemies,
" than to their complaisant friends, as they fre-
" quently heard the truth from the one, but never
" from the other." Now as I have already observed that it is incompatible with human nature never to err, the most adviseable conduct for us to pursue is, to search carefully into our own hearts, and if, upon an impartial self-examination, we find ourselves really guilty of the faults laid to our charge, let us endeavour to amend, if not, strive to avoid them. Thus Plutarch says that, whenever any thing is alledged against us that is not true, we ought not to despise and neglect it because it is false, but should carefully examine which of our words or actions has given a specious handle to the calumny, and cautiously guard against a similar conduct in future* for the wise and prudent, as the same Philosopher

* " When Plato was told, that his enemies were busily employed
" in circulating reports to his disadvantage, he said, *I will live so,*
" *that none shall believe them.*' And Diogenes upon some one's asking him, how he might revenge himself upon his enemy? made answer, *by being yourself an upright and honest man.* Brucker's *Hist. of Philosophy*, B. ii. Ch. xii. S. i. Plut. de Cap. ex Host. Utilit.

observes, know how to make a good use of the malice of their enemies. Such wisdom and such prudence let it be our strenuous endeavour to attain, for however paradoxical the assertion may seem, there are many cases wherein an enemy is a blessing*. *Melmoth's Lælius, p* 125--6 *Plut. de Capiend. ex Host. Utilit.*

* Thus Philip of Macedon used to think himself indebted to the Athenian Demagogues for their liberal abuse of him. For, says he, *I will endeavour both by my words and actions to prove them Liars.*

Plut. Apophtheg.

FINIS